NORTHERN VIRGINIA
LUMINARIES

JOE MOTHERAL

THE
History
PRESS

Published by The History Press
Charleston, SC
www.historypress.com

First published 2023

Manufactured in the United States

ISBN 9781467153164

Library of Congress Control Number: 2022949524

Dedicated to my wife, Marjorie, family and friends.

CONTENTS

CONTENTS

INTRODUCTION

My wife, Marjorie, and I moved to Northern Virginia, specifically Leesburg, in 1998. At the time, it was mostly rural compared to today's intense development, particularly in eastern Loudoun County. Northern Virginia itself was a combination of urban and rural components. Its proximity to Washington, D.C., Dulles Airport, the native origins and its pleasant countryside surroundings made it an attraction for many families. We consider ourselves fortunate to live in this environment.

The trigger that set off a chain of events involving meeting and being able to interview interesting people was the *Loudoun Times Mirror*. The editor at the time was Martin Casey, who liked having stories about historic or interesting roads in Loudoun County. As a freelance writer, I had been assigned to write about Edwards Ferry Road, which is rife with history. The road at one time ran all the way from Leesburg to the Potomac River at the intersection of Goose Creek. It connected with Edwards Ferry, which operated from the 1700s until around 1920. The Union forces during the Civil War marched down Edwards Ferry Road to cross the river on their way to Gettysburg. There are Civil War trenches on the Sage Hill Farm and an old ordinary, plus a park with stone structures that used to be part of a farm.

When the *Times Mirror* published the article, we received a note from Eeda and Alfred Dennis in the gatehouse entrance to the River Creek community, where we lived. The note asked us to call them. Their home—Sage Hill, with farmland—is located on Edwards Ferry Road. We made the phone call and became friends. The Dennises had lived in Leesburg for over thirty years and, as a result, knew a wide range of people. They were kind enough to get us involved with their friends, and because of that, we were able to expand our knowledge and acquaintances, some of whom are included in this book.

Because of the Dennises, we were able to meet and get to know Russell Baker and his family. Eeda and Alfred invited us to attend a fundraiser in Bluemont; Baker had volunteered to be the main attraction. We met both Russell and his wife, Mimi. In the coming weeks, Alfred Dennis arranged a weekly luncheon at the Eiffel Tower Restaurant in Leesburg. Knowing Russell gave us a ripple effect. He introduced us to Pat Sloyan, James Reston Jr., Jim Lehrer and Roger Mudd.

The Dennises got us into a dinner group that met monthly at rotating homes. This group included others who had a presence in Northern Virginia: Joan Williams, Alice Scheetz, Kitty Weaver and Albert Ward. In addition, Eeda being a big fan of George C. Marshall got us involved with the Marshall Center in Leesburg.

According to a representative of the National Sporting Library and Museum in Middleburg, sometime in the 1920s, there was a fox-hunting competition between the United States and the United Kingdom to take place in the vicinity of Middleburg and Upperville. It apparently was a highly publicized event all over the world. And the United States won! As a result, wealthy families—the DuPonts, Kennedys, Mellons, Jack Kent Cooke and more—bought land in the area. A number of members of the horse community followed and spread out in Fauquier, Clarke and Frederick Counties.

Northern Virginia is a bedrock of American history even before the Civil War, with plantations that were connected with the British colonies. In Northern Virginia, you have Oatlands, for example, in the National Trust for Historic Preservation. When the Eustis family owned it, they hosted the Roosevelts, and General George C. Marshall kept a horse there and occasionally could be seen riding horseback.

Early in our living in Leesburg, we noticed a magazine named *Grapevine* that was placed in some of the restaurants. It was formatted like a newspaper but had local entries—sightseeing, points of interest, people, restaurants and so on. It was based in Frederick, Maryland. I decided to get in touch with the publisher, Donna Elbert. We met, and I began writing about people and places for the magazine. They arranged an interview with Robert E. Simon, the founder of Reston. As time went on, I became "Closeup" editor, dealing with profiles of well-known people in the area. Later, *Grapevine* shut down, and then after a couple of years, Donna initiated *Eastern Home and Travel* magazine, and I was able to do some travel and cultural pieces.

The other door that opened involved the National Press Club. In 1999, shortly after we moved to this area, an old friend of my folks, John Cooper, sponsored our membership into the National Press Club. I joined the Book and Author Committee, which hosted the annual book fair, when one hundred authors came with their books. The event was open to the public so people could come in and meet the authors, buy books and have them signed. That gave me the opportunity to meet Roger Mudd and others such as Jim Lehrer, Eleanor Herman, Michael Crichton, Andrew Young, George McGovern and more. Eleanor Herman was also a member of the Book and Author Committee.

Another member, Judy Pomeranz, wrote for *elan* magazine, based in Great Falls, Virginia. She connected me with *elan*, and I had the privilege of writing for them, mostly about artists—thanks to Judy. It was a special pleasure to get to know and work for David Reynolds, the publisher, and Jean Davis, the editor.

They were kind enough to give me some assignments. Others included Hulya Aksu, publisher of *Posh Seven*, and Len Shapiro, publisher of *Country Zest* and *Style* magazines, edited by Vicky Moon. I also continued with the *Loudoun Times Mirror* and its publisher, Peter Arundel, and its several editors over the years. Thanks to Bea Snyder, who published several stories in *Reflections Magazine*. I am thankful to all of them for publishing stories I wrote about Northern Virginia luminaries. Major credits also go to The History Press and Kate Jenkins and Hilary Parrish, who have been most effective people to work with. Credit goes out to the many family members of those deceased who provided photos and information.

But with all of this, the biggest thank-you goes to Eeda and Alfred Dennis, with whom we had wonderful times. This is especially true as this book relates to Northern Virginia. We would occasionally go driving around the area with them, and they would give us a running account of people they knew as we passed one house after another.

Chapter 1

RUSSELL BAKER

2004, 2005, 2010

Introducing Russell Baker

Russell Baker has lived in Leesburg for the better part of thirty years. He was born in Morrisonville, in western Loudoun County, and then went on to the *Baltimore Sun* as a reporter. Following that, he joined the *New York Times* staff and eventually won a Pulitzer for his column "The Observer." He was handed another Pulitzer for his book *Growing Up*, about his childhood in Loudoun County. For anyone living here, it should be a must-read. He spent twelve years as host on *Masterpiece Theatre*, writing his own introduction. In addition to these prestigious credits, the National Press Club honored him with the Fourth Estate Award.

At age ninety, he decided to hang up his writing after an illustrious career. He could often be seen walking the streets of Leesburg for exercise. He passed away at age ninety-three.

An Evening with "The Observer"

Baker gave a talk at one of the middle schools some while back. He kept his audience in stitches with his commentary on writing and the English language.

One of his favorite books as a child, he said, was *Treasure Island*. The one scene he remembers vividly was when the crew threatens Long John

Russell Baker. *Photo by Joe Motheral.*

Silver with mutiny. They give him a piece of paper with a black spot on it. The only paper they had was a page out of the Bible. "Long John Silver, surrounded by cutthroats, stood his ground and shamed them by referring to their blasphemy, thereby thwarting the mutiny. Good stuff," Baker said.

> *Radio was the thing when I was growing up. We didn't have TV then. Radio stimulated your imagination with sound effects and dialogue. I remember listening to episodes of the* Lone Ranger *and how I imagined him wonderfully in my mind. When TV came along, here was this man wearing long johns and a Halloween mask. What a disappointment.*

He talked of once wanting to be a novelist like Ernest Hemingway. "I came to realize that writing like Hemingway had already been done—by Hemingway. Writing novels doesn't pay much, and you have to eat. I wrote a novel once and years later recovered the manuscript and threw it away."

He poked fun at the picture of a lonely writer:

> *They go into a room every morning and close the shutters and roam around inside a darkened room and inside their skull for three or four hours, then that's*

it. Exhausting business. Especially exhausting if you roamed around in my skull. This process can be interrupted occasionally by your wife asking you to run an errand to the supermarket. No wonder all these famous novelists— Hemingway, Fitzgerald, Sinclair Lewis, Steinbeck—drank to excess.

He dealt a glancing blow to some writers' use of English: "Womanizing. Um, we don't 'manize.' It's womanizing here and womanizing there. He was womanizing, they were womanizing, we were womanizing. What does it mean? Would the future perfect be 'will have been womanizing'? To womanize? I suppose it's because we can't say 'ladyize.' It's amazing, this 'nouning of verbs.'"

He spoke fondly of journalism: "It's being on the ground. Reality. Meeting and being with interesting people and events. I used to cover the Senate and would sit in the press box every day. Could even go to the sergeant-at-arms and ask to see Everett Dirksen or Lyndon Johnson, and they would come out for an interview. Of course, they would talk but not really say anything."

Someone asked him why he returned to Loudoun County after spending some of his childhood here.

The landlord kept raising the rent in New York, where we had lived for eleven years while I worked for the New York Times. *When we lived in Loudoun County as a child, my mother kept referring to the place as "the sticks." But we had to leave New York and drove down here. When we did, we thought, "Hey, it's beautiful here. This is the most beautiful place we've seen!"*

All in all, the evening was entertainment from an eminent man of journalism—like radio, better than TV. As Hemingway might have said, it was "a moveable feast."

Growing Up

In the book *Growing Up*, Russell Baker's Pulitzer Prize–winning autobiography in part about his youth in Loudoun County, chapter 2 starts out, "I began working in journalism when I was eight years old," which he says was prompted by an admonition from his mother to "make something of himself." Thus began a nearly eighty-year odyssey that first took him to the *Baltimore Sun* as a police reporter and finally returned him to Loudoun County and Leesburg, where he now lives in a brick home of 1800s vintage. During such a long journey, he made intermediate stops to write columns, books and articles, all the while snagging legions of loyal readers and serving as a television host for *Masterpiece Theatre* from 1994 to 2005. He now says he's in "deep retirement." His profession rewarded him with two Pulitzer Prizes, numerous other awards and a membership as a fellow in the prestigious American Academy of Arts and Sciences.

He was the *Sun*'s London correspondent and White House correspondent from 1947 to 1954. In 1954, he joined the *New York Times*, and in 1962, he began writing his column titled "The Observer." In the introduction of his book, "There's a Country in My Cellar," he describes when he started the column and the terrifying feeling of having to deliver three columns a week. If he heard the voice of panic, he either ignored it or dealt with it effectively, because he wrote it unfailingly for thirty-six years.

The book *Growing Up*, published in 1989, has within its contents the enduring capacity for discovery and rediscovery, especially for residents of Loudoun County.

He described Loudoun County the way it used to be:

> *My father was a stone mason; oldest brother was a contractor who did work for the railroad. People went to work in the morning with a lunch pail. Everybody wore overalls. They did work with their hands. They built things. That's gone from Loudoun County. Back then we had modest lives and modest homes. People had cattle and everyone had a hog which was butchered every November as a community thing.*

He mentions with a sense of nostalgia occasionally driving over one of the stone bridges in Loudoun County that his father built.

His grandmother had a small garden and raised beans, beets, potatoes and corn. She canned enough to sustain them through the winter. The whole county was mostly farmland, where wheat was the major crop. That way of life has been replaced by high-priced real estate and seemingly no room for low-cost housing. Frequent trips to the area to visit his son, Michael, along with a renewed love of Loudoun County, pulled Russell and his wife into Leesburg almost twenty years ago, when the town, ironically, was more urban than it is today and more so than Morrisonville, where he spent his childhood. "Mimi's [his wife] a city girl," he said; back then, everything, including a supermarket, was within walking distance of their house.

It was journalism that took him away from that previous age in the county. Even though *Growing Up* gave him fame as a book writer, he said, "I'm a journalist, a newspaperman and always have been. That's the way I started." It would only be natural, then, that his most satisfying body of work was "The Observer." "The column was a lot of my life. After it was all over you wonder if it was worthy of the man." In an extended moment of self-analysis, he said, "Some of it was pretty good. Some of it was awful. If you write that much, some of it is bound to be awful.

"But it was satisfying, and I made good money at it and in such a showcase as the *New York Times*—the world's greatest showcase. Everybody reads it—everybody you would like to have read you."

He indicated that he probably wouldn't write another book. He said he had a couple of ideas, but if he were to act on them, "I probably wouldn't be talking to you now," he said with a chuckle. "I'd be working."

He offered two reasons to write a book. One is to do so for a great deal of money, and the other is because you "just gotta write that book." That's the way it was with *Growing Up*. He wanted to write a book about people no one knew—his family, with his uncles he described as "characters." He said he had the great good fortune to have this large family, and he wrote the book as if seeing through the eyes of a child. It was so successful that one publisher came to him wanting him to write another one, offering him $1 million. After he accepted, he said he caught himself thinking, "I can't write a book that's worth that much money." The book, *The Good Times*, he says wasn't as good as *Growing Up*.

He was influenced by Max Shulman—although he doesn't like to admit that now—James Thurber and Hemingway.

The two Pulitzer Prize certificates hang in the corner of his office—one for *Growing Up* and another for journalism. Their significance seems hidden by their simplicity.

He said the journalists of his time lived next door to policemen and firemen in blue-collar neighborhoods. Don Graham of the *Washington Post*, for example, served as a policeman in Washington for two years. Baker told young journalists of today to "work without health insurance."

A Trip to Morrisonville

The settlement of Morrisonville straddles the intersection of Morrisonville Road and Purcellville Road in western Loudoun County. True, it has rural character, but it doesn't appear to have much else to distinguish it—except that one of Leesburg's most prominent citizens came from there. Russell Baker drove us in his Toyota Avalon west on Route 7 before turning onto Route 9 through Paonian Springs. He then turned north on Highway 287 and began to talk about the area: "This is extremely rich farmland. Wheatlands (only a sign these days) is mentioned in British eighteenth-century agricultural literature as a place that produces marvelous corn—as they called wheat. When I was a kid, they grew wheat and corn up here."

He pointed westward toward the Short Hill Mountains and Harpers Ferry. He paused thoughtfully for a moment. "John Brown's last recorded words as they were taking him out on a cart to the gallows were, as he looked around, 'I never realized before this place was so beautiful.'"

In a short distance, we turned left on Morrisonville Road. He said it was a dirt road when he was a kid and he remembered seeing Model Ts buried up to their hubs after a rain. "Like a winter scene in Soviet Russia."

His uncle Irvey became the chairman of the county supervisors and, with that power, had the road paved in the '50s. "They didn't want paving because you have a nightmare there, and Uncle Irvey is to blame for that."

We pulled off the road briefly at his son Michael's house with its springhouse and log structure. Then we drove on a ways. "This is Morrisonville proper. Michael lives in what I call the suburbs."

He talked of the place where he was born near the southwest corner of the intersection; the surrounding wheat fields; his cousin's father being a butcher by trade; and where they used to butcher cattle to sell the beef. His cousin and he would participate and end up "taking the guts out in the field for the vultures. It was an awful bloody spectacle." He said it was an exciting time then but now "would make me sick." There was an apple orchard down there, he said, gesturing toward the field below the house. "We used to play baseball there."

"Everybody had at least one pig that was the winter's food supply." The butchering took place in November, and as he said, "It was a communal activity. Friends would come and go from house to house. They had a calendar. They would block off the dirt road and set up tables with huge black cauldrons. It was exciting," he said with a smile. "The luxury of country life."

After his father died, his mother moved her family to New Jersey. The first year, there was a polio epidemic in the early '30s, and his mother sent him to live with his grandmother and to attend school. "I went to a two-room school. I was in the room with first, second and third grades. I started in the first grade, but by the end of the year, I had finished three grades." Queried about the location of the school, he laughed and said, "The school was up the road a 'right good piece,' as they used to say. It could be fifty yards or twenty-five miles."

He returned to Morrisonville during the summer occasionally in the '30s until his grandmother died. He pointed to a house that stands on high ground overlooking the intersection. "There, that house that looks like a Swiss chalet. It was my grandmother's house. It all came down, but they built something on the footprint." He indicated another place across the road where he lived once and another place where "Old Mr. Ben Cooper's house has fallen on bad days. I remember he had a parrot."

He spoke of his grandmother Ida Rebecca Baker. "She had thirteen children, twelve of them boys; one girl—we called aunt sister. They were staggered. They used to go to work at age thirteen." He smiled and said, "She was a marine sergeant. She didn't put up with much." He said, "My Uncle Irvey was sort of the prime minister. But he was always deferential around my grandmother."

We came to a T intersection. "Down that road they had church picnics in the summer on Sunday afternoons." We noticed the road named "Picnic Road." "It was wonderful," he said. "Bandstands. All the men wore white shirts and neck ties. The women brought fried chicken, homemade cakes, ice cream dips, crackerjacks. That's where I had my first cigarette, under the bandstand at the church picnic."

Continuing on westward on Morrisonville Road, we passed the schoolhouse that had been torn down and in its place a residence probably built with the same stone. In those days, native stone often was the chosen construction material. His father, Benjamin, had been trained as a stonemason, as had his uncle Irvey. We passed what then was a baseball field where town teams played, the Zion Lutheran Church and a grove of trees on the right. "I went with my father one time—because it's where the bootleggers were—to buy hooch. I just remember sitting in the Model T and a lot of men standing around joking."

We moved on Route 287 toward Lovettsville, where he said, "We could get an ice cream cone. But at one time there was a store in Morrisonville, in fact two stores. It was competition—capitalism." He mentioned that they had a trial there with the judge sitting behind the grocery counter. "Someone had shot someone's bull." Beyond Lovettsville across the bridge over the Potomac, you came to "paradise—Brunswick. People didn't go to Leesburg. They went to Brunswick." He remembered his mother talking about one of her students, saying with anticipation that a trip to Brunswick would be a lifetime experience.

For his book *Growing Up*, he interviewed a number of family members who were still alive then, including Uncle Irvy, at that time age ninety. Russell said that they played hard in those days—the 1890s. "Drinking, rough humor. They would steal chickens then have a card game and eat fried chicken."

We drove into the cemetery at the New Jerusalem Lutheran Church in Lovettsville. A number of gravestones bear the name Baker. "There's my cousin Berkley. Cousin Walter over there." Also buried there are his grandmother Ida Rebecca, whose birth date was actually 1861 instead of 1860, as inscribed; father Benjamin; and Uncle Edgar, who managed the Morrisonville baseball team. It almost seemed as if the entire population of Morrisonville was gone. But most certainly, a wealth of memories remains, and what better guide than Russell Baker to visit them.

The beginning of this journey that included Russell Baker was because of Eeda and Alfred Dennis, who had retired from the State Department and sold real estate, including the house he sold to the Bakers in Leesburg. When we went with the Dennises to the fundraiser for firemen, we met the Bakers—Mimi and Russell. In a conversation with Mimi, I mentioned that we were looking for a carpenter-type person who could make a fireplace mantel. She gave me their phone number and said to call her the next day so she could give me the name of someone.

I phoned the next day as she suggested, and she gave me the name and phone number of the carpenter. Then off the top of my head I asked, "Do you suppose Russell would like to go to lunch sometime?"

"Oh yes, yes, please. He needs to get out of the house."

That and mainly the connection with Alfred started fifteen years of weekly lunches with Alfred, Russell and Jack Wilson, and later with Keith Wauchope in place of Jack after he passed away.

Keith had spent a career with the State Department, including being ambassador to Gabon. Occasionally, Russell introduced us to others he knew by inviting them to lunch: Roger Mudd, Jim Lehrer and Pat Sloyan. Initially, we would meet at the Eiffel Tower restaurant on Loudoun Street in Leesburg. Later, we changed from week to week.

As a result, we learned a lot about Russell's career. He told one story about having an interview with President Lyndon Johnson: "While we were talking, Johnson wrote a note on a piece of paper, then called his secretary in and gave it to her. When we finished the interview, I walked out and stopped at the secretary's desk and asked what was that all about. She replied, 'He wanted to know who in the hell is this I'm talking to.'"

In one of his books, he included an essay titled "A Summer's Day" about when he was a kid with a buddy spending time together on a day in the summer. After nightfall, they were sitting outside when a meteor crossed the sky. Russell's friend said, "You can make a wish on that." Russell replied that he did not know that and "I didn't have a wish to make."

———

Published in *elan* magazine, *Loudoun Times Mirror* and *Reflections*. *Russell passed away in January 2019 at age ninety-three.*

Chapter 2

KITTY WEAVER

2006

To know the road ahead, ask those coming back.
—Chinese proverb

Miles of world is better than reading ten thousand scrolls of books.
—Chinese proverb

Don't tell me how educated you are. Tell me how much you have traveled.
—Muhammad

Aldie is a small town, a village really, along the shores of Route 50 in Northern Virginia. On the edge of horse country, just down the road from Middleburg, it has little to lift it out of obscurity except maybe the Aldie Mill, a preserved nineteenth-century edifice, and except for one of its residents, Kitty Weaver. My trip took me south twenty minutes or so from Leesburg, the county seat of Loudoun County, down Route 15 to Gilbert's Corner, the intersection of 15 and 50, and thence to Aldie, where Kitty lives on some acreage in a house about the same age as Aldie Mill. Kitty has made a career of travel, and to know her is to know something about the world.

She has visited 135 countries, including forty-eight trips to Russia. One of her most memorable experiences she relates was having lunch with kangaroos in Australia. "One grabbed a sandwich. They looked like E.T. when they stood up. They would tap us on the shoulder as if they wanted something, then they wandered off and took a nap."

Kitty Weaver. *Photo by Joe Motheral.*

She was on Russian TV when a Russian theatrical troupe came to New York, as they wanted to ask Kitty what she thought of their performance. By then, she had previously spent months in Moscow, which she says is her choice for the most interesting place, including going to Moscow University to study philosophy. "It was the philosophy of communism. I was in a class of students under thirty-five who didn't know the past." She speaks Russian and had completed the course work for a PhD at Georgetown University in Russian studies and was ready to write her thesis when her professor said, "Why don't you write a book instead?" She did: *Lenin's Grandchildren*, the story of preschool education in Russia. Finishing her PhD would have to wait.

Her Russian language capability stood her in good stead once in Uruguay. As she says, "I travel by myself, never in a group. You meet people that way. In a group, you are cordoned off." She met a woman in Montevideo who tried Spanish on Kitty. Kitty caught enough to understand that the woman was originally from Poland. Then Kitty spoke in Russian, and the woman got all excited and said over and over, "Russkya, Russkya!" She invited Kitty for lunch in her new apartment equipped with maid service and all. Kitty says the woman kept spilling something on her dress, and the maid stood by with a spray bottle, which she applied every time the woman spilled.

She says though that "Dayton, Tennessee is the friendliest place I've ever seen." She has been working on a book about primates and visited Dayton to attend the reenactment of the Scopes Trial.

I got to the airport and found out there were no taxis. They told me the courthouse where they were having the reenactment was three miles away. I had to walk. I started out walking and walked about a mile when a police car stopped me. The policeman took me into town but to the wrong place. "I'll drive you to the right place," patrolman Tracy Blevins said. "I'll drive you back to your motel." He had talked to his superior, and he said to take me anywhere I wanted to go. So for two days he took me sightseeing.

That was four or five years ago, she said. "We went to the police station, and one of his fellow policemen thought I was a prisoner and came over to help process me."

She talks of visiting Indonesia, where she encountered a group of orangutans on the Island of Sumatra. "One of them grabbed me. At first I was complimented. Then he started biting [softly] like a puppy playing. The attendant had to hit it with a stick. The orangutan wanted me to roll around on the ground with him. But I didn't want to." She laughed.

One year, she went to Petra, the ancient city carved out of the cliffs and defiles in Jordan. She rode a donkey into the city. "You know a donkey goes where it wants to go. We rode along the edge of the mountain. It would hit a stone that would bounce down the side of the mountain. It was scary. We got there anyhow. They had to pick me up and put me on the donkey."

Kitty is a slight woman who draws easily on her travel experiences and said at one point that her next trip will be to Machu Picchu in Peru. Maybe that doesn't seem so ambitious—unless you consider her age: "I just had my ninety-fifth birthday."

Lately, she amended her travel objective to Easter Island. She said, "Maybe too much walking for me at Machu Picchu. For the first time, I'm starting to feel old." She went on to talk about the course she was taking twice a week at George Washington University about Russian cinema. That's after she had a daily walk for thirty minutes on her treadmill, followed by twenty minutes in her exercise pool.

She had play time too. She belonged to the Middleburg Tennis Club, and as Ms. Weaver's niece-in-law Patsy Dunlap remembers, "Aunt Kitty decided she wanted to ride horses. She started taking lessons, but long before she finished, she revealed to her instructor that she was already riding in fox hunts. The instructor was mortified."

She was an active member of the Fauquier Garden Club, the Virginia Garden Club, the Aldi Horticultural Club, Sulgrave Club, Metropolitan Club and Chevy Chase Club.

At one point, Weaver and her husband raised chickens, and according to Patsy, they sold and delivered eggs to the Red Fox Inn. Patsy said, "She kept detailed records, and I ran across this when going through her belongings."

Middleburg was also the launching pad for her worldwide adventures. It was there that she became interested in Russia and began taking Russian language lessons.

She hosted the Kennedys once when they called her asking if they could visit and see her dog. They were getting ready to acquire one and wanted to check hers out. Weaver recalled, "John John was just a little boy, and he went around outside our house picking up acorns."

Kitty Weaver passed away in January 2013 at age 102.

Kitty Weaver (1910–2013)—Obituary

Ms. Katherine "Kitty" Weaver, an exceptional woman in Aldie and Loudoun County; active in local and statewide organizations; a Russian scholar; author of three books about Russia: *Lenin's Grandchildren*, *A Bushel of Rubles* and *Russia's Future*, passed away Friday, January 11, of complications from pneumonia. Ms. Weaver was 102 years old.

She had an insatiable curiosity that led her to travel to 135 countries during her lifetime; to attain the academic requirements for a PhD in Russian area studies at Georgetown University; and to attend William and Mary for a bachelor of arts degree and a bachelor of science degree in agriculture from the University of Maryland. She even spent months as a student at Moscow University. She was a friend of the world and enjoyed meeting and getting to know people from all walks of life.

Ms. Kitty née Katherine Dunlap was born in Frankfort, Kentucky, on September 24, 1910, and when she was three years old, she and her parents moved to St. Petersburg, Florida, where her father wrote a daily column for the *St. Petersburg Times*. Later, while at William and Mary, she met Henry Byrne "Hank" Weaver, whom she married. He subsequently became an established Washington attorney. Eventually, in 1947, they made their home in Aldie. Mr. Weaver died in 1995.

Her yen to travel and to learn about the world and its people began at an early age. Her adventures included being the first American ever to visit a small village in China; riding donkey back at age ninety-three in Petra, Jordan; and meeting a Polish woman in Uruguay with whom, to the woman's surprise, she spoke Russian and they had dinner together. A lover of animals, she has communed with orangutans in Indonesia and kangaroos in Australia. She once said, "I like to travel alone rather in a group. You don't get cordoned off that way, and you meet people."

One she met was Winston Churchill—both on a book tour in Denver, Colorado. When she asked him where he was going next, he replied, "Some little town in Virginia you probably never heard of: Middleburg." Another time, she met Fidel Castro. She knew the Kennedy family and had dinner with Eleanor Roosevelt, whom she said took off her shoes while dining.

Her world view most assuredly included the local scene. She was an active member of the Fauquier Garden Club, the Virginia Garden Club, the Aldi Horticultural Club, Sulgrave Club, Metropolitan Club and the Chevy Chase Club, and after she had passed the age of ninety, she attended classes in anthropology in Washington, D.C., as well as taking courses in Russian cinema at GWU. Her passion for literature never left her, as she was in more than one local book club. Ms. Kitty was writing her fourth book when she died: *You Don't Get to 100 Overnight*. She was a steadfast volunteer of the Hospital Ladies Board, a philanthropic organization where she received honors for her work.

She was one of Willard Scott's television centenarians in September 2010.

A friend of hers said that when she was young as part of the Middleburg milieu, she engaged in fox hunting and loved to play tennis.

Ms. Weaver specified in her will that there would be no memorial service. But all her many friends and admirers have to do is remember her zest for life. That alone is a tribute and a memorial.

She is survived by her nephew William Gray Dunlap, who with his wife, Patsy, has stayed with Ms. Kitty since 2005.

Published in *Grapevine Magazine* and *Middleburg Life*

Chapter 3

MARY HARRIS

2007

Occasionally on a hot summer afternoon, if you drive along Edwards Ferry Road east of Leesburg in a stretch of rural Loudoun County, you might see a slight woman with a hose on the edge of the road spraying water to keep the dust down. If you've been around awhile, you know that woman is Mary Harris, who is the matron of Cattail Farm. She's delighted these days, as the section of road next to her place has been paved and she doesn't have to maintain the dust level anymore.

Since she moved to the farm over fifty years ago with her husband, Huntington Harris, the rural nature of her surroundings has seen enormous changes that have increased the traffic on Edwards Ferry Road tenfold. But inside her home, with her four dogs and her penchant for tending her garden out back—a plot on her 150-acre land where the farm's namesake Cattail Run wends its way to Goose Creek—she hardly notices the turmoil outside.

None of this opens any window to her past—one that she says she enjoys talking about. She retains her British accent and seems to delight in telling stories of her experiences. Her blue eyes liven and the creases in her face become almost animated as she sits her slight eighty-six-year-old frame in her favorite chair.

She was born in 1921 as Mary Hutchison in Shanghai, China, of English and Scottish parentage. At the age of three, she and her father, a British diplomat, and her mother left Shanghai. "You see in those days, British diplomats served three years overseas, then returned to England for six months."

They eventually returned to China. Many British children customarily were sent to boarding school at a comparatively early age by American

Mary Harris. *Photo by Henry Harris.*

standards. But at eight years, Mary would have none of it. "I objected and refused to go." So they all went back to China.

The Hutchison name in Hong Kong is well known. There is, for example, a Hutchison House office building. And Mary says her family was connected to the Hong Kong Shanghai Bank—a prominent institution in China. These roots go back to the 1860s, and she says, "My grandfather was a missionary in China. He translated the English Bible into Chinese."

Her grandfather, according to Mary, was in Hong Kong when he heard a woman's beautiful singing voice. "He eventually married the beautiful singing voice."

"I'm hopeless with dates," she says as she talks about being in Peking, Hong Kong, Harbin and Shanghai with no particular chronological reference. But sometime in the 1930s, when they were stationed in Harbin, northern China, the Japanese invaded. "We lived on top of a hill and weren't bothered. We knew one woman from another diplomat family with two children who got shot in the back."

At some point later, they found themselves again in Shanghai. Then in December 1941, the Japanese occupied the city. "It was strange," she says, "this one day, the Japanese authorities gave us until 11:00 p.m. to destroy all of our secret documents." By then, Mary, age twenty, was working in the British Embassy as a coder. "They took us to a hotel along with the French and Dutch diplomats. The food wasn't very good. But we used to go out and buy peanut butter."

She describes her "incarceration" as relatively benign. "I would go to the desk where the guard was and tell him I was going out, and he would say okay. But when my parents wanted to go out, they were allowed to walk only around the hotel. That was it."

The setting in China during that period was anything but stable. There was the fall of the Manchu Dynasty, the founding of the Republic of China by Dr. Sun Yat-sen and Chiang Kai-shek, a graduate of Whampoa Military Academy who took the mantle of leadership by forming the Nationalist Party (Kuomintang) after Dr. Sun died. But he had to subdue the warlords and deal with Mao Zedong and his Communist Party. On top of that, you had the Japanese incursion into China. They bombed cities in China, occupied key areas and wrought havoc on the population.

In 1942, the diplomats and their families in Shanghai boarded Japanese ships bound for Africa, while Japanese internees went aboard British ships. They met in Portuguese East Africa, a neutral country, where they made the exchange. Mary says she continued her job as a coder in the British consulate in Lourenço Marques, the capital. There, she met her future husband, American Huntington Harris. Malcolm Muggeridge, a prominent name in the United Kingdom, headed up the section of MI-5 where Mary was stationed.

Muggeridge initially had been attracted to Communism and spent time with his British wife in Moscow in 1932. There, he worked for the *Manchester Guardian* as a journalist. He later became disenchanted with Communism; wrote a couple of novels; became a radio and television personality; and, finally for our story, joined the British Secret Intelligence Service, first in Brussels and later in Lourenço Marques. According to some reports, the intelligence he gathered was responsible for the capture of a German U-boat. Mary said:

> *We were mostly keeping tabs on shipping traffic between Japan and Shanghai. Huntington was there with the Office of Strategic Services (OSS). He shared a house with Malcolm, who introduced us, and so we had plenty of time to get to know each other.*
>
> *The British people said, "We don't want you marrying an American," and the Americans said, "We don't want you marrying a British." They were afraid, you see, that we would have access to each other's secrets, which was nonsense. Hunt told them he wouldn't let me see any secret papers.*

They somehow resolved the question, and Huntington and the twenty-one-year-old Mary were married. "Soon afterward, Hunt was transferred to British West Africa. I quit my job and went with him."

They eventually moved to the States. Mary was pregnant with their firstborn when Huntington was reassigned to Italy while the war was still going on. "I lived in St. Paul, Minnesota, with Hunt's brother and family while he was away."

After the war, they came to Virginia, where Huntington's father owned property. "Huntington acquired the adjacent property from his sister where we are now."

The road outside Mary's house that once led to Edwards Ferry on the Potomac has its own claim on history, as it bore troop movements during the Civil War and one of the buildings on her farm was once known as Cattail Ordinary, an old inn consisting of two buildings connected by a common roof—all vintage eighteenth century. The space between the buildings was reserved for carriages to come and discharge their passengers. A British subject—Nicholas Cresswell—who, it is said, had the distinction of missing the last boat to England at the outset of the Revolutionary War, mentioned in his journal that he dined and stayed overnight at Cattail Ordinary. The original building was partly destroyed by fire, although Mary said some of the logs from the old inn remain.

Huntington Harris had quite a distinguished career in Loudoun County— as a supervisor, entrepreneur and active participant along with Mary in community service. He was chairman of the board of Paxton Home for Children and was voted Citizen of the Year in 1975 for public service. He passed away in 1993.

Mary's move to Loudoun County gave her a liking for horseback riding. She said, "A friend taught me how to ride here (different than in England). I had a horse named Daybreak because," she said, chuckling, "I used to get up and ride him at daybreak."

Her housekeeper, Linda, asked if we wanted any more iced tea. One of her dogs, ten-year-old Friday, whom Mary says was so named because she found him on a Friday, came over and put his head on my knee. Mary stirred and went over to a table laden with photo albums. Glancing through them, we relived in miniscule graphics the past she had been telling us about with pictures of a young Mary in China. Soon, it was time to leave her to her farm, her gardening and her memories.

Published in *Grapevine Magazine*
Mary Harris passed away in 2012.

Chapter 4

PAT SLOYAN

2007

I 've always had a nose for controversy." So says sixty-nine-year-old Patrick Sloyan, two-time Pulitzer Prize–winning journalist whose pastoral surroundings at his home in Paeonian Springs, Virginia—a short sprint from Leesburg—seem to say otherwise. The domestic venue expands when you consider that several of his six grandchildren live next door and he and his wife, Phyllis, spend daily quality time with them.

We walked out behind his house and toured his eight-acre property, a plot of land originally bordered by a stone fence—a good indicator of age. He boards a couple of horses, one thirty-seven years old; has a fair-sized garden and two barns, and across the road in a separate building he has his office, where wall plaques and photos represent a journalistic past and a forty-year career that included his coverage of national and international affairs for United Press International, Hearst News Service and *Newsday*.

He was awarded the Pulitzer Prize in 1992 for international reporting on the first Gulf War. He uncovered American casualties involving friendly fire, deaths and injuries hidden from reporters, "blocked by the command from witnessing combat." He reported as well on tactics against the Iraqi army that could well have given "pride" a bad name—stuff he says the military was less than enthusiastic to talk about or even disclose. His stories were poignant reminders that war is not a pleasant experience.

The road to journalistic prominence began, he says, in January 1955. "I joined the army after the Korean War to get the GI Bill. I ended up—got training—as a combat engineer and started by putting out the battalion

Pat Sloyan. *Photo by Phyllis Sloyan.*

newspaper." Later, after being assigned to duty in Germany, his apprenticeship continued when he was handed the job of producing the divisional newspaper. "I wrote news stories. In those days, we had the draft and, as a result, a well-educated caliber of people. The army taught me everything about putting out a newspaper. I had a great time."

One army story involved a cook who was court-martialed after he ignored an order to stop serving potatoes to hungry troops in the field. "I wrote about it." The story ended up in *Time* magazine and with a Pentagon investigation. The cook was subsequently cleared.

Once Pat got out of the army, he says his first job was with the *Albany Times Union* in Albany, New York—a Randolph Hearst newspaper. Then, in 1959, he decided to attend the University of Maryland on the GI Bill. A delay in government tuition payment forced him to scramble for money. So he says he joined the swim team for a scholarship that included meals.

Before graduating in 1962, he worked as a student in the university's Public Relations Department and was a stringer for the *Washington Star* and the *Baltimore News Post*. Then one day, he says, the UPI bureau chief visited the campus, where the chief's daughter was attending classes. One thing led to another, and Patrick soon was working at UPI. "It was good training and an art form. You learned to be accurate and fast on the biggest and most complicated stories." And he says, "If you were thirty seconds late on a competitive story with the Associated Press, you got talked to. You couldn't make three mistakes and stay on the job."

He stayed with UPI until 1969. One time, he says, "I got a phone call from the White House. It was Lyndon Johnson." It seems there was a published story about Johnson's ranch near Johnson City, Texas, indicating that the ranch had been opened to the public for "fee"—an apparent misprint of the word "free." Johnson told Patrick to get it corrected. As usual, Patrick double-checked and made the correction.

I asked him what he thought his most interesting story was. He talked about his coverage of when Ralph Nader took on the auto industry, incurring their wrath and at the same time touching the conscience of a nation. "It got ugly," he says. "The Capital Police caught a guy stalking Nader." Turns out, he had been hired by General Motors, whose president came before a congressional committee later and apologized. "The whole thing was, GMC, Ford and Chrysler knew their cars were unsafe. Because of Nader, we have restraining devices and other safety features in cars today that have saved untold numbers of lives."

After leaving UPI, Pat joined the *Newsday* staff and in 1986 became its Washington bureau chief. His career has spanned nine presidents, twenty Congresses and twelve presidential campaigns. He covered the 1962 Cuban Missile Crisis; the 1963 assassination of President John F. Kennedy; the Vietnam War; the civil rights struggle; Watergate; Iran-Contra; and, as London correspondent, the Israeli invasion of Lebanon and British invasion of the Falklands. He's won numerous awards, including a second Pulitzer in 1997 for being part of the *Newsday* team in the spot news reporting category on the crash of TWA 800 off the coast of Long Island. Some of his dispatches have turned up in college textbooks as examples of model reporting. Aside from "daily journalism," he has had his work published in *Rolling Stone*, the *New Republic*, the *Nation*, the *Washington Monthly*, *American Journalism Review*, the *Washington Post Outlook* and the *London Guardian*.

Patrick was born in Stamford, Connecticut, and graduated from Cathedral High School in Indianapolis in 1954. His name is common in Ireland's County Mayo and has its origins in the Gaelic word for army assembly points—maybe an early hint of things to come.

I asked Pat what makes a good reporter. He said, "Curiosity and a desire to understand." That and his nose for controversy have given him present-day causes. He's been fighting to keep power lines from being constructed along the WO&D historic trail right-of-way. He recently had his letter published in the *Washington Post* advocating the transmission lines be constructed underground. His latest campaign involves what he describes as the gradual demise of newspapers owing to corporate bottom lines: "They've closed foreign bureaus and have laid off many of their senior, most experienced reporters and editors. What used to be the best American newspapers have dropped investigative journalism for warm and fuzzy features."

Patrick says Merriman Smith, formerly of the UPI, was his idea of a skilled journalist. Smith reported on the Kennedy assassination from the scene.

Besides his interest in ensuring that the public knows the real story, Pat has taken time out at least once a year to visit his brother in California and play golf with the likes of the movie actor William Devane and in the past with someone who became his friend, none other than Gerald Ford, who was his news source during the Warren Commission deliberations.

As we concluded the interview in Pat's office, I noticed a chess board. "Oh that. I'm teaching the grandkids to play chess."

———

Sloyan's last effort as a journalist and writer was his book *The Politics of Deception*, published in 2015 about the Kennedy administration based on 260 tapes he was able to review. It contains interesting information and revealed facts about the Cuban Missile Crisis and the Vietnam War.

Pat was devoted to his family, which included grandchildren living next door to him and Phyllis. The name *Sloyan* is listed in the library in Dublin as an Irish name. As such, he always enjoyed an occasional Guinness.

———

Published in *Grapevine Magazine*
Patrick Sloyan died on February 4, 2019.

Chapter 5

JOAN WILLIAMS

Joan Williams lived at Little Oatlands until her death in 2014. She was a member of the Beauregard family. Her parents died in 1927, and she became the ward of David and Margaret Finley. David Finley was Andrew Mellon's attorney. That gave her access to places and people with famous names. At the same time, she led her own colorful life. She was an accomplished artist and gardener, was active in the local garden club and sang in the Episcopal church choir. Joan served on the board for a number of years at Oatlands, the plantation south of Leesburg that is well connected with the history of the area.

For example, when she was a teenager, she met the Roosevelts at Oatlands, shortly after FDR had a historic meeting with Winston Churchill. And as she grew older, the list of the famous also grew to include Ethel Kennedy and Barbara Bush (both of whom played tennis with her), Lady Astor, Douglas Fairbanks Jr., the Trumans and others. When Joan was twelve years old, she spent time at the White House. "This was in 1939. Roosevelt's granddaughter was there, and he wanted her to meet some people."

Joan attended Foxcroft Boarding and Day School near Middleburg during the Second World War, when she said, "The royalty and upper class in England sent their kids to the States to attend Foxcroft." She mentioned in particular Davina Bowes-Lyon. "Her aunt was the Queen—not the present Queen, the Queen's mother." And she said the Duke and Duchess of Windsor came for a visit once. Joan was at Foxcroft from 1941 to 1944. She later attended Bryn Mawr and Sewanee.

At one point in her life, she was in a horrific auto accident in which she banged her head on the windshield. I asked her how this had affected her life. Surprisingly, she replied, "I realized I didn't have to please everyone anymore."

She once spoke about her great-uncle Confederate general P.G.T. Beauregard, who was stationed in Savannah, Georgia, when the Union forces under General Sherman swept in. Joan said that she had heard that "General Beauregard turned over his house to the Union forces because he didn't want it destroyed."

She was a tennis player in her younger days. She played tennis with Ethel Kennedy, who she says "played tennis while chewing gum. I didn't like that very much." She also played

Joan Williams. *Photo by Richard Williams.*

regularly with Barbara Bush. Joan said, "One day Barbara came to the court crying. Turns out she had had some kind of emotional episode."

Joan's friend for thirty years, Eeda Dennis, said of her, "She was a faithful friend—I always enjoyed her. She had a lot of spunk." Eeda commented that she loved Joan's paintings and that she had some hanging in her house. She went on to say that the garden at Little Oatlands is "beautiful, planned by David and Margaret Finley with trees and sculptures in perfect harmony." The Little Oatlands garden has been featured several times during Virginia Garden Week.

Andrea McGimsey, who was executive director of Oatlands, said that Mrs. Williams was a long and faithful supporter of Oatlands over the decades. Among other things, she donated a historic piano that belonged to the Eustis family. "Joan loved Jane Austen and named her two Jack Russell dogs after Austen characters. We love Joan and her family, and they are in our thoughts and prayers. We are so grateful to Joan. We miss her."

During the one year we recorded Joan's memoirs, we were able to extract some memories. Lori Kimball, who at the time was president of the Loudoun Preservation Society, attended several of our recording sessions as well and was able to bring out Joan's intense interest in Oatlands. William Eustis, an avid equestrian, found the location ideally suited for fox hunting; Ms. Eustis, enchanted by the neglected gardens, was determined to return them to their former splendor.

Joan Williams with husband and friend. *Photo by Richard Williams.*

When Mrs. Eustis passed away in 1964, her two daughters, Margaret Eustis Finley and Anne Eustis Emmett, donated the Oatlands mansion, its furnishings and 261 acres around it to the National Trust for Historic Preservation.

Today, Oatlands is a self-supporting co-stewardship National Trust Historic Site. The mission of Oatlands is to preserve the property for future generations, interpret the house and grounds to the public and serve as an educational resource. The grounds also are available for special events and private functions.

Some conversations follow with Joan Williams. "LK" is Lori Kimball; "JM," Joe Motheral; "JW," Joan Williams.

Joan Williams's
garden. *Courtesy
Richard Williams.*

LK: How did you meet Dick? Have you recorded that already?

JM: Yeah, but go ahead.

JW: I met him on Lehigh Place or whatever the name of the place is off of Connecticut Avenue with Rollie Evans. Rollie is the one who wrote with Joe Alsop.

JM: Lady Astor? I thought she was British?

JW: No, she was American and she was married to an American and divorced him and then married the British Astor—I don't know whether it was Waldorf or not—and then she became, she was in, what do you call it, not the Lord, the other. She was the first woman in the…

JM: House of Lords?

JW: Queen Elizabeth Sr., not the current Queen Elizabeth. Her mother.

JM: Oh my gosh?!

JW: Her name was Davina Bowes-Lyon, and her aunt was the queen.

JW: This was the fall of 1950.

JM: 1950

JW: We hadn't met him yet. Well Dick knew him well, so he was the one that was in charge of marrying us for this little group. This very special little group, the Scroll and Key. I met him, and then we went to his apartment for the night because he was going with his wife to have a baby with her parents in Connecticut. So he was taking her up there. I don't know how all this was going to be, but that night he left his apartment empty for us so…

JM: So you stayed there?

JW: He runs for the mayor, and that was very exciting, and we were very involved in that. Trying to get money in Washington.

JM: Were you really?

JW: We were even carrying money the day after they had the election; we were carrying money we had gotten in the elevator.

JW: We stayed at Gracie Mansion.

JM: You stayed at Gracie Mansion several times?

JW: Three, four or five times. There was a special coming-out party for their oldest daughter. We were there for that. There were other things that came up that we got to go. It was just fabulous.

JW: I was twelve.

JM: Twelve years old. What did you think of Roosevelt?

JW: Well, I was really impressed.

JM: What did you do with her?

JW: We had lunch, and then I met with him personally after lunch.

JM: Did you meet General [George] Marshall?

JW: Oh yes, I did when he was having tea with Mrs. Eustis at Oatlands. Several times during the war. Uncle David was an attorney. [Uncle David] met [Mellon] when [Mellon] was secretary of the treasury. Uncle David was an attorney in the Treasury Department.

Joan Williams passed away in 2014.

Chapter 6

ELEANOR HERMAN

2008

McLean resident Eleanor Herman, best-selling author of *Sex with Kings* and *Sex with the Queen*, has tackled another controversial subject in her latest venture, *Mistress of the Vatican: The True Life of Olimpia Maidalchini, The Secret Female Pope*. The subject of her biography is the sister-in-law and possibly the mistress of Pope Innocent X. From the pope's 1644 election until his death in 1655, Olimpia directed Vatican business, appointed cardinals, negotiated with foreign ambassadors and helped herself to a heaping portion of the state treasury.

Born in humble circumstances and almost locked up in a convent at fifteen, Olimpia married first for money and, finding herself a rich young widow, second for a noble title. A domineering woman, she managed the career of her well-meaning but indecisive brother-in-law, Gianbattista Pamphili, helping him rise to the papal throne as Pope Innocent X. But life wasn't easy as first lady of Rome; she endured public hatred, a squabbling family and a group of cardinals who vowed to elect an enemy of hers in the next conclave, a pope who would punish Olimpia for her many misdeeds.

Reviews have been generous: a starred *Publisher's Weekly* review reported the book was "exhaustively researched with historical vignettes interwoven seamlessly. Herman's latest provides a window into an age of empire; nepotism and intrigue that rivals any novel for fascinating reading." Kirkus Reviews called it "an incredible life of a formidable woman, fetchingly told." The *Catholic Review*, while doubting some of her conclusions, said,

Eleanor Herman. *Photo provided by Eleanor Herman.*

"Herman has an engaging style and creates an interesting read about Maidalchini, Rome and the state of the church at that time." One Catholic was less enthusiastic. On August 27, a man apparently leaving the Basilica of the Assumption on Cathedral Street in Baltimore threw a rock through the Enoch Pratt Library window featuring Eleanor's book poster.

Eleanor shrugged off the vandalism incident:

The Catholic Church has a rich and colorful 2,000-year history, going straight back to Jesus. It is not reasonable to expect all popes and cardinals in such unforgiving times to be saints; they were very human. And from about 750 to 1870, the pope was also monarch of a kingdom called the Papal States. Sometimes the Vicar of Christ was in the unenviable position of having to defend his territory by leading an army against hostile Catholic nations. Can you imagine Benedict XVI climbing into a tank to attack, say, Venice? The church has corrected many abuses of former times and is in a much better position today, able to concentrate on spiritual matters. Whoever threw that rock must have had a bit too much communion wine.

What abuses were corrected? Eleanor explained:

Until 1904, the conclaves leaked like sieves, messages going in and out daily, while on the street bookies changed the odds for each cardinal. Cardinals didn't have to take holy orders; until 1917, they could decide to leave the Sacred College and get married. Most shockingly, when a pope lay dying, his servants pillaged his rooms, stealing even his blankets and candles as he lay shivering in the dark. As soon as he died, they came back and stole the bed. And the pope's family was supposed to pay for his funeral, as they had stolen every last penny from the Vatican treasury to buy themselves palaces. In Innocent's last days, his sister-in-law managed to steal the entire Vatican gold reserve.

Eleanor researched in various Italian archives, as well as in the Folger Shakespeare Library in Washington, which possesses a large cache of seventeenth-century Vatican documents. "The hardest part of the research was deciphering the handwriting," she said. "And the language was sort of Shakespearean, with few rules of spelling and punctuation. And then there were the abbreviations I had to figure out!"

Her goal was to create a book that was the closest thing to time travel, exploring not only one woman's fascinating life also but the art, architecture, politics, church affairs, etiquette and household management of the time.

I found a 1660 book written by a butler on how to manage a cardinal's household and many others on their really scary health care, not to mention hundreds of books on theology and church history. My favorite was an early etiquette book which advised, "And when thou hast blowne thy nose, use not to open thy handkerchief, to glare uppon thy snot, as if thou hadst pearles and Rubies fallen from they braynes." I think that advice would be useful to anyone today.

Eleanor also worked with a D.C. psychologist, Dr. Adi Shmueli, to get into the minds of her main characters. She said of him:

He has an uncanny ability to know people without seeing them, just by hearing a few stories about them. I figured if he could do this with living people, he could do it with dead ones as well. He helped me immeasurably in truly understanding what motivated Olimpia, and in having compassion for her, even when I didn't like the things she did.

In Italy, Eleanor found Olimpia's previously unknown birthplace and the registry of her birth. Like many women, Olimpia had lied about her age. Eleanor visited her palace in Rome's Piazza Navona, now the Brazilian Embassy, and her city of San Martino fifty miles north, where she gave 250 houses to dowerless girls, as she had once been, so they could avoid the convent or a life of prostitution. "She was extremely generous to women in need," Eleanor said, "but could exact excruciating vengeance on anyone who crossed her, even if it took thirty years."

Eleanor's love for history was jumpstarted by a family tree that goes back twenty-eight generations to her namesake, Eleanor of Aquitaine, and forty-four generations to Charlemagne. She even named her black Labrador puppy Charlemagne—Charlie for short. Her journey began in Baltimore, where she majored in mass communications at Towson University. After working for various local publications and studying German and Italian in Europe, she worked for thirteen years with Bonn-based Monch Publishing as associate publisher for North America for *NATO's Nations and Partners for Peace* magazine. More recently, she hosted episodes of *Lost Worlds* for the History Channel and has appeared in *The Madness of Henry VII* for the National Geographic Channel and has been on history channels in Germany and Italy.

Eleanor's next book, *Murder in the Garden of God*, should prove every bit as entertaining. It takes place in the 1580s during the reign of the brilliant Pope Sixtus V. She said, "Picture something like Hamlet in the Vatican: murder, adultery and revenge. I couldn't make up a better plot. I adore the pope's character, though no female character could ever compare with Olimpia."

Will she ever write history about earlier periods, or is she stuck in the Renaissance and Baroque? "Earlier ages have fascinating stories," she said, "but suffer from a lack of documentation. Once you hit about 1500, there are lots of diaries, letters and diplomatic dispatches. I like to let the people of the time speak for themselves."

LEGACY OF KINGS, 2016

Eleanor Herman left a trail of best-selling nonfiction books and then wrote *Legacy of Kings*, a novel about Alexander the Great. As she said, "I always wanted to write fiction—to create entire worlds and have the power of life and death at my fingertips." In writing about Alexander, she said, "People started writing about Alexander when he was twenty years old and his father, Philip, was assassinated. Before that, his life is almost blank. It's fascinating as a novelist to create his world, his challenges, his hopes and fears at the pivotal age of sixteen."

The lead into the book reads, "Imagine a time when the gods turn a blind eye to the agony of men, when the last of the hellions roam the plains and evil stirs beyond the edges of the map. A time when cities burn, and in their ashes, empires rise." The initial chapters introduce the main characters and their interactions with one another, all of whom had ties to Philip of Macedon's royal court in Greece. Alexander, Macedon's sixteen-year-old heir, is on the brink of discovering his fated role in conquering the known world but finds himself drawn to a beautiful and mysterious peasant girl, Katerina, "who must navigate the dark secrets of court life while keeping hidden her own mission: kill the queen." Jacob (a fictional character) wants Kat and will do anything for that purpose, especially to preempt Hephaestion, who is a murderer but the best friend of Alexander. Then there is Zofia, a Persian princess and Alexander's "unmet betrothed."

Herman chose Alexander "because he was a pivotal character in history who led tens of thousands of men into India and would have probably led them to China if his men hadn't mutinied because they wanted to go back home."

The book leads the reader into the primary battles and involves the women whom Herman dresses in armor in preparation for meeting the enemy. The description of the clashes of the armies comes from Herman's intensive research. From her previous works of nonfiction and her historical knowledge, she had a basic understanding of "the ancient Mediterranean world." "I researched pretty much all aspects of life all over again to make sure I got it right: food, clothing, transportation, politics, warfare. Researching ancient warfare was most interesting for me. I read several works written thousands of years ago on strategies used to win battles."

This will be the first in a series of four books on the subject of Alexander, all taking place in the fourth century BC. According to history, at age eighteen, Alexander assisted his father, Philip, in defeating the Athenian and Theban armies at Chaeronea. Following the death of his father, he took over the Macedonian army, conquering Persia and Egypt, and eventually his kingdom extended to the border of India. He has the reputation of being a brilliant military leader and a powerful ruler.

Herman makes use of repeated descriptions that give that dimension of humanness to her characters, an example being when Alexander enters a tournament in which he does battle with other individuals: "Alex licks his lips and tastes salty sweat creep into his mouth, but he cannot pause even for a moment to wipe his face. He needs every ounce of concentration just to keep up with Lord Bastian, let alone to defeat him."

Eleanor's latest project involves the country of Ghana in Africa. She got acquainted with recently nominated King Peggy, who has responsibility for a specified area within the country to collect taxes and settle disputes. Eleanor has a book in the works about King Peggy and already has received an advance payment from a publisher. She plans to donate part of that money to improve potable water resources in King Peggy's territory. There is talk of a movie and that Queen Latifah has expressed interest in playing King Peggy.

The combination of four books has been picked up by Warner Brothers Television for a TV series, and a script writer is already at work. Herman is no stranger to television, having appeared on the Discovery and History Channels, along with National Geographic and the American Heroes channel, contributing her expertise as a historian. Her previous four books all deal with historical nonfiction: *Sex with Kings*, *Sex with the Queen*, *Mistress of the Vatican* and *King Peggy*. History remains her thread with the novel *Legacy of Kings*, and Alexander the Great is certainly a historic figure.

———

Eleanor Herman has been a longtime member of the Book and Author Committee at the National Press Club, where she has appeared to discuss her books. Her latest books include *Sex with*

Presidents and *The Royal Art of Poison*. In the fall of 2022, her book *Off with Her Head: Three Thousand Years of Demonizing Women in Power* was published.

She said, "The book examines what the patriarchy, throughout time, does to women who step on their 'space,' which is usually the kitchen." She cites examples: Cleopatra, Anne Boleyn, Marie Antoinette, Hillary Clinton. "They are often criticized not for political decisions so much as for their appearance, for being sluts, witches, bitches, unfeminine, too ambitious, unlikable and untrustworthy. It's hard to believe this kind of thing has been going on for thousands of years."

Eleanor gave lectures at the History Book Festival in Lewes, Delaware, in September 2022.

And more in the future? "I have several TV and movie options in the works for my books and look forward to consulting on scripts, meeting with Hollywood executives and that kind of thing." Her fingers are crossed that she will be able to succeed. As she describes, "Taking a book to TV or film is extraordinarily complex."

In the past, she has presented her books at Politics and Prose in Washington, D.C.

———

Published in *elan* and *Posh Seven*

Chapter 7

DARRELL GREEN

2001

Darrell Green of the Washington Redskins and resident of Ashburn will be a cinch for the professional football hall of fame. But he should be awarded society's hall of fame nomination for his Youth Life Foundation—learning centers where underprivileged kids, ages five to eighteen, can get academic help and help with their lives.

He describes his own experiences as a youngster in Houston, Texas, that led him to help the kids of today:

> *I think my father was my role model when I was growing up. He was the male that was closest to me and the most influential in my life. It was just a good relationship. He was strong and very vocal. I used to come home from school, and we would wash the car together and do things together. I think every kid is predisposed to his or her father, and if you spend time with that person, he will have a voice or influence in your life. So from zero to ten, I spent a lot of time with my dad, and that influenced me the most and had a real impact in my life.*

He and his family then were churchgoing people, but Darrell says he really didn't know the Lord until later in his life. Likewise, he says, there was no single moment in his young life when he had an epiphany—some experience or revelation that motivated him to form his learning centers.

> *I can't point to a moment. It was the way I was raised; the way our mother taught us to care for other people. Then when I came into the league, I*

Darrell Green. *Photo by Washington Football Team.*

became a Christian and got a credibly broader view of service for good. I just think we were always taught to treat people right; taught to look out for the less fortunate. We were taught to give; to serve; to respect others; and we were taught to share. I think it was my whole childhood, not any one moment. My parents taught me that you're not an island; there are more people on this earth, and you need to be responsible for more than just yourself. My mother would give her last dime serving people.

His foundation has learning centers in Washington, D.C.; Tennessee; North Carolina; and at the Loudoun doorstep in Berryville at the Johnson-Williams Middle School, where John Scott, a fifth-grade teacher from Boyce, supervises four mentors and seven or eight kids between fifth and twelfth grades. They meet two days a week in the afternoons. The mentors are athletes from Shenandoah University and receive pay for their work with the kids. Scott said:

These young men from Shenandoah are screened just as if they have applied for a teaching job at any school. The kids for the most part are at-risk kids and come from single-parent households. They all struggle somewhat with academics. We start with their homework, but most important is their interaction with a male role model. We do one hour of academics then a half hour of sports. I think the main thing these kids get out of this is self-esteem.

Pat McDonald, third baseman and pitcher at SU, sits with his two charges and guides them in their science and math homework.

Darrell Green talked about the makeup of these centers. "This isn't a volunteer mission. This is professional work. We want professional teachers, professional administrators and professional leaders. We're not offering our kids a secondhand service. We don't take 286 computers and put them in our labs."

He and his family like Loudoun County because it's close to Redskins Park and it has an excellent school system and a small-town atmosphere. He looks small for a pro football player, but he has stature—ask any wide receiver who has come up against him or any kid who is a product of one of his learning centers.

Darrell Green, the all-pro corner back of the then–Washington Redskins, along with Dan Snyder, the Redskins owner, gave a luncheon talk at the National Press Club in December 2001. I located Green's publicist, gave her my card and asked if I could get an interview with him on behalf of the *Loudoun Times Mirror*.

About two weeks later, she called and invited me along with three other reporters to Redskins Park for an interview. I raced out to FedEx Field in Landover, Maryland. Once I was there, while talking with several staff and trying to locate Darrell Green, no one knew anything about his being there. So I phoned the publicist, who said, "I said Redskins Park in Ashburn. I can't guarantee he will be here."

I jumped in the car and raced to Redskins Park, which is about ten minutes from where we lived. I walked into the stadium, and Green was seated in a chair waiting. I couldn't believe my good fortune. He was very nice and accommodating. He even had a TV crew waiting to interview him, but he gave me time without seeming impatient. J.B. Brown of the TV crew asked me, "Who are you anyway?"

I replied, "I'm nobody." To this day, I can't say enough about what a gentleman Darrell Green was. He was perfectly within his rights to put me off. But he didn't.

Published in *Loudoun Times Mirror*

Chapter 8

HELEN ZUGHAIB

2014

Helen Zughaib's "Soaring Spirits" series of paintings has been given favorable reviews by the *Washington Post* art critic, who wrote, "The selection includes some pictures that have been exhibited before, on themes that include dreams, the roles of women and the history of Western art. They reflect not only her passion for art but her recognition of the ideals she says this country represents."

Helen explained that her first artistic inclination was inspired when she lived with her parents in Paris. Matisse influenced her work, along with artists who painted Persian miniatures. Born in Beirut, she came with her family to the United States in 1977. She attended Syracuse University, where she received a BFA at the College of Visual and Performing Art in 1981.

Once in the States, she almost immediately acknowledged the freedoms that gave her the incentive to portray that in her artwork. "The George Washington Monument is part of a series I painted after coming to live in Washington, D.C. The monuments are so impressive in their meaning and ideals."

So impressive, in fact, is the Washington Monument that it was selected by the State Department for Secretary Clinton to give to the king of Morocco in 2009. Another of her paintings, titled *Midnight Prayers*, President Obama presented to Prime Minister Maliki of Iraq at the White House in August 2009.

Each of her paintings has a Middle Eastern flavor. The shapes and colors augment a distinctive style that can't help but attract attention and study. Her blending of East and West seems to express a global sense of unity. A good example of this is her painting *Prayer Rug for America*, which she says "was in an exhibition that opened at Meridian International Center in February 2002 following the tragedy of 9/11." She says, "That painting was my attempt to bring together East and West in a portal of spirituality and reflection." The exhibition garnered much publicity, including from both CBS and CNN; each network interviewed Helen, as well as several other artists included in the exhibition, about their reactions to 9/11 as reflected in their work.

Helen Zughaib. *Photo by Basil Kiwan.*

Helen's painstaking attention to detail requires long hours each day in her studio on Virginia Avenue in Washington. She says that it usually takes four to six weeks to complete a painting, and she concentrates on one at a time. Her medium is what she calls "opaque watercolor, or gouache." This type of paint is "very unforgiving and dries quickly." According to her bio, the use of gouache and ink on paper tends to "transform her subjects into a combination of colors and patterns creating a nontraditional sense of space and perspective." This technique is very evident in most all of her work. Many of her paintings employ a latticework of multiple colors that contribute to her distinctive style.

She showed me the pencil-thin brushes she uses and says she has to replace them frequently, as they swell a bit and lose their point each time they are used.

Helen has a feel for symbolism. One of her paintings consists of a dark-haired woman with a shawl over her head peering into a hand mirror that reflects a blond-headed woman minus the shawl. Helen told me its meaning is how the woman regards herself in an entirely different image.

She does take a break occasionally and goes jogging on the National Mall, a fitting venue for her monument series of paintings. While the popularity of the monuments has given her gravity in many circles, she also has done a series of twenty-three paintings titled "Stories My Father Told Me." These paintings accompany her father's narratives from his early childhood in Damascus, Syria, and young adulthood in Lebanon before eventually coming to America.

George Washington Memorial, by Helen Zughaib. It was given to the king of Morocco by Secretary of State Hillary Clinton on behalf of the American people. *Photo by Basil Kiwan.*

Midnight Prayers, by Helen Zughaib. It was given to the prime minister of Iraq by President Barack Obama on behalf of the American people. *Photo by Basil Kiwan.*

She is now concentrating on an Arab Spring series. As part of this series, she has painted a number of birds with flowing colors called *Spring Flight*, which was exhibited in the SYRA arts gallery in Georgetown by its founder and good friend of Helen's, Sylvia Van Vliet-Ragheb, who says she is opening a gallery in McLean, where she will continue showing Helen's paintings. One eye-catching canvas had a grouping of multicolored domes and minarets depicting Middle Eastern countries with a blue sky in the background. Helen said, "The blue sky represents hope. Hope that these countries will someday find peace."

She explains further, "My work on this series ['Arab Spring'] attempts to express my feelings of beauty, sadness and hope for the future of the Arab world."

Sylvia at the art gallery has a high opinion of Helen's art: "I believe Helen's work distinguishes itself from other Middle Eastern artists. She likes to engage in modernistic styles, taking from modernist masters like Picasso, Leger and Mondrian, while using distinctly local and traditional theme, which then creates a unique visual language." She goes on to describe people's reaction to her paintings: "People are taken by her style and the vibrant colors she uses. Her pieces are very happy."

It's little wonder that her artwork has been exhibited worldwide with acclaim from East and West in the form of a number of awards.

Washington, D.C. resident Helen Zughaib has just been given a three-year Kennedy Center/REACH Residency. She says, "I was nominated to talk about women, migration and refugee crises. And will have a big show in June that coincides with International

Refugee Day." This fits with the themes in many of her paintings, as she says that she is inspired by the events in the world. "I feel I have a responsibility to record those in paintings."

Published in *elan* magazine

Chapter 9

ALAN GEOFFRION

2012

I was heading south out of Middleburg, Virginia, toward The Plains one Monday not too long ago when my cell phone rang. "Hello, this is Alan. It's Monday, and the Rail Stop is closed on Mondays. Let's meet there though, and we can go to another place I know."

We had originally agreed to have lunch at the Rail Stop in The Plains—a restaurant once owned by famed movie actor Robert Duvall. It seemed appropriate at the time since the sixty-year-old Alan Geoffrion of Warrenton is a neighbor and has been a friend of Duvall's for thirteen years. Alan also wrote the screenplay for the television miniseries *Broken Trail*, starring Duvall.

I had previously met Alan at one of the Waterford Foundation's lecture series at a session when he discussed the making of *Broken Trail*. Since then, we had arranged to get together for an interview.

I followed his pickup along Route 55 west toward Marshall before turning in where there is a building marked "Livestock Auction." There was no livestock today but a cozy café where many of the patrons seated at the counter and those behind the counter knew Alan. After a BLT, French fries and a glass of iced tea, we set out on a tour of the auction house. Alan remembered, "Years ago, I used to come here to look over the horses." Alan and his wife, Danielle, have been owners and breeders of horses for some time. It seemed natural, as the miniseries *Broken Trail* was all about moving horses from Oregon to Wyoming. But as he would tell you, it was about more than that.

Broken Trail was his first screenplay, based on his book by the same name. It all started, he said, when one day over lunch with Robert Duvall, he told him about this place in San Francisco where young Chinese women were sold into bondage. At the same lunch, he talked about his fascination with horses that had been driven to be sold to South African interests for service in the Boer War. "Bobby told me to write it down." That was it. A year later, it was a television miniseries nominated for two Golden Globe Awards.

Alan Geoffrion. *Courtesy Alan Geoffrion.*

I asked him the difference between writing a screenplay and writing a novel. He responded, "A screenplay is mostly dialogue. You leave out as many descriptive passages as possible—no long, flowing descriptions. And you have to always be thinking of production costs." He said in many ways, he prefers writing a novel because it's less restrictive.

He cited an example of being sensitive to production costs. The filming of *Broken Trail*, he said, took place in forty-five days in Canada, where the government has been encouraging filmmaking to the point of giving a rebate. In the case of *Broken Trail*, which cost $14 million to make, the Canadian government returned $2 million. There was one scene he said that entailed the herd of some two hundred horses to be situated on the side of a mountain in exceptionally rugged terrain. "The head wrangler came up to me and said, 'That's pretty rough; we are going to have to shoe the horses.' And at $75 a head, it would have amounted to around $15,000. Not only that, but we would have had to pay extra for the camera crew and production crew. So we looked around and found another less rugged spot that served the purpose just as well."

Generally, he said, screenplays are about 100 to 120 pages to form an hour-and-a-half film. He thinks there's a lot of packaging these days. It's all about money; as one of the characters in his book says, "Money greases the wheels." He said, "I don't think there's a connection between money spent and quality of product. Having to live within a tight budget, I think, keeps the creative juices firing."

He admires screenplay writer Horton Foote and, in fact, sent the original screenplay of *Broken Trail* to him for comment. Foote, who wrote the screenplays for *To Kill a Mockingbird* and *Tender Mercies*, thought that Alan's being relatively inexperienced was a good thing—no built-in biases.

Broken Trail is set in 1898 with two main characters: Prentice "Print" Ritter (Robert Duvall) and Tom Harte, played by Thomas Haden Church. Ritter wants to square some family problems with his nephew, and toward that end, he proposes to purchase five hundred mustangs and transport them from Oregon to Wyoming to be sold to the British army. In the meantime, complications set in when Ritter and Harte encounter a white slaver who owns five Chinese girls. The two rescue the women, and as a result, the woman who owned them hires a gang to follow them and recover the women. The story mostly involves interaction among the various characters rather than physical action, although there is some of that too. For example, Harte is Ritter's estranged nephew. On the trail drive, they get to know each other. A Mrs. Nola Johns (played by Greta Scacchi), an abused woman also rescued by the team, falls for Ritter.

The screenplay went through evolutions, as Alan explained: "The studio wanted more action. Bobby wanted more in the way of character study." During the filming, Alan, who remained with the filming the entire time, would make changes in the script and slip them under the actors' doors at night. "I would see Duvall the next morning when, as Bobby described it, 'we'd practice quiet anarchy.'" Who made the biggest contribution to change? "I'd have to say Bobby because he had the power. All we did mostly was change it back to the way it originally was."

Alan said, "We didn't have to come up with a lot of new stuff. I met with the Chinese girls when I got up there. I told them, 'Look, I'm just an old white man, and I don't know much about girls and I sure don't know much about young Chinese girls, so if there is anything in this script that you feel contradicts or is untruthful, you let me know.'" He went on to say, "Bobby was up for that. He likes things loose and quiet."

From my own experience of having lived in Taiwan for a number of years, I thought the Chinese culture portrayed in *Broken Trail* was accurate.

Alan's original title was *Daughters of Joy*. A focus group came up with the title *Broken Trail*. Alan said at the time, "It doesn't mean anything!" "That's what we like" came the reply—purposely ambiguous for fear of offending somebody.

Alan said, "I felt that in this story, there was a double meaning to [my original] title because these little girls become kind of the daughters of the uncle and nephew. Although it doesn't end happily for all of them, there is a certain amount of joy."

Alan is writing a prequel to *Broken Trail* that goes back to China. It's about political and social upheaval and famine and follows the character Huang He to San Francisco and the fate of the girls. Alan said, "I do a lot of reading and research—sometimes half a day." Then he says he would like to do a sequel by following the horses to Capetown and the Boer War. He is working on another one set in Texas.

I asked him if he had any parting thoughts. "I don't mean to sound high minded. Everybody has one story in them. I encourage people to write it down. I think it's very therapeutic. Perhaps a family incident in your life."

He seems to like the simple things. When he comes to Leesburg, for example, he prefers to dine at Leesburg Restaurant, a workingman's eatery. "I like their peanut soup and the country ham."

***

Alan Geoffrion was nominated for a Golden Globe, as was Duvall, who was so awarded. Alan participated as one of the one hundred or so authors at the annual National Press Club's Book Fair in 2012 or 2013. The night before the big event, he called me and said, "I'm bringing Bobby." He was referring to Robert Duvall.

Duvall came in with Alan and, of course, was an immediate hit. He was very cordial and impressive. He looked just like his image in movies. Most of the staff at NPC are Hispanic. Duvall went around and spoke to them in Spanish.

Alan explained that at the movie set, the cast has a linguist whose job it is to give them an accent from their home origin. One of the cast members in *Broken Trail* is supposed to be from Virginia. He went to the linguist and asked for a Virginia accent. The linguist replied, "Which one? There are six."

***

Published in *elan* magazine

Chapter 10

ALICE SCHEETZ

2002

I remember the first time some twenty years ago that I drove up the lane that must stretch half a mile toward the river off Edwards Ferry Road, winding gradually to the right and rising, framed by cedar trees and zigzag split rail fences. The stately two-story residence, made completely of native stone at the hands of an expert stonemason, presides over a peaceful view of the tip of Harrison's Island, with Sugarloaf Mountain in the distance and a sweep of rolling pastureland, forest and farm buildings.

Alice Scheetz lit the fire in the Colonial-style fireplace and settled in her favorite chair in the quiet of a living room appointed with memorabilia, family photos, paintings, portraits and shelves filled with books. She had passed the age of ninety, but she graciously made no concession to age.

Why, Edwards Ferry Road was just a dirt road when my father, Mr. Rust, bought this property and built this house in 1938. When it rained, it was awful. We bogged down in the car. Finally, the county—I believe it was the county—came out and put stones in the road. They would sink after a bit, then they would come put more stones.

An Admiral Moffit owned this property, fifty-eight acres, before us. He used it for hunting.

We first raised chickens, turkeys and guinea fowl, but there were too many red foxes, so we gave that up. My father grew tired of seeing white feathers all around the place. The original land included River Creek, which we later sold.

Alice Sheetz. *Photo by John Rust.*

She pointed to the floor next to the fireplace. "Someone found those three stone cannonballs down there somewhere near the river."

"I remember hearing stories about the Indians when I was a little girl. Harrison Island was the place where they gathered to make treaties. Later, there was a farm holding there, a woman who had barges to cart cattle and other things back and forth across the river. She used to have parties with bright lights on her barge."

She recalled the previously mentioned Nicholas Cresswell, the Englishman who stayed at Cattail Ordinary. "I don't have any personal knowledge of this, mind you," she said with a smile and a twinkle in her eye, "but I think he got stuck here during the Revolutionary War and was here for quite some time. No one bothered him. He just kind of drifted." Indeed, that excerpt from his journal indicated as much.

Alice Scheetz's grandfather was a colonel in the Civil War, and her great-grandfather came from England and owned Rockland Farm—still in the family—at the other end of Harrison Island. She remembers her great-grandfather only as a man of "substance."

Peggy and Alice Scheetz's nephew John Rust now resides at Murray Hill, so named for John Rust's grandfather. John said, "There is also a Murray Hill in Pittsburgh where my grandfather lived."

With some exceptions, such as the houses on Cattail Run Farm, stone and stonemasonry held sway as the dominant building material. According to Professor Charles Poland, a historian from Northern Virginia Community College, "Stone houses had their genesis in Pennsylvania, and many of them started out as log cabins. Later on, wood siding would be added, followed by a covering of stone."

John Rust thinks that the stone for his house and other similar structures including the Dennis home came from Luck Stone Quarry, which he says was operating in the 1930s. The quarry is located in Loudoun County.

Stonemasonry, whose origins defy the breadth of time, has become a lost art. But evidence of these artisans has been maintained along Edwards Ferry Road, where the past abounds. These monuments and the people involved give us a glimpse into that past.

Alice Scheetz passed away in 2005.

Chapter 11
ARTHUR GODFREY

2019

Introduction

In 1946, radio and television star Arthur Godfrey purchased an elaborate home just west of Leesburg in Paeonian Springs. He was noted as an entertainer from Manhattan who spent much of his career in television and radio in Loudoun County. He was trained as a pilot in the navy and often flew back and forth between here and New York. His lifespan (1903 to 1983) included most of that time in Loudoun County. Remembered as the "Old Redhead," he would often pull out his ukulele and sing, "In the Blue Ridge Mountains of Virginia on the trail of the lonesome pine. In the pale moonshine our hearts entwined when you carved your name and I carved mine."

Radio, Television and Recordings

One of his most notable shows on CBS was *Arthur Godfrey and His Friends*, preceded by *Arthur Godfrey's Talent Scouts*. The list of famous people he had on his show is endless. They are mostly names from the past that have been etched in entertainment history: Pat Boone, Tony Bennett, Rosemary Clooney and Eddie Fisher. Country and western singer Patsy Cline, who came from Winchester, had a spot on his show. Despite the fact that he apparently passed on having Elvis Presley as a guest, his show was rated number two next to *I Love Lucy*. Eventually, it did go down in the ratings, but in its day, it was quite popular.

All of his shows took place at his home in Paeonian Springs. In order to facilitate doing this, he had a microwave tower and a studio built at his home. His shows were live, and according to some sources, he often tossed his script and winged it. Apparently, the sponsors loved him, as he used their products and could speak from experience. Lipton Tea was one of his favorites. One example: Godfrey wavered from the script and said, "Aw, who wrote this stuff? Everybody knows Lipton's is the best tea you can buy. Water and the tea and let it just sit there."

Arthur Godfrey. *Photo from Guideposts.*

In addition to his TV and radio appearances, he also recorded songs. Among them was "Too Fat to Polka," which reached number two on the charts in 1947. He also recorded "I'm Looking Over a Four-Leafed Clover."

Leesburg Airport

Godfrey flew each week back and forth between Leesburg and New York. According to one local resident who lived in the area during Godfrey's time, there was once a runway on Edwards Ferry Road from where it intersects today with Route 15 Bypass toward the center of Leesburg. At the time, the area now occupied by commercial and residential entities was barren. He initially flew a single-engine plane but later bought a DC-3, and the town objected to its size and potential danger. In addition, Alfred Dennis said, "People objected to the noise." Some described it as "rattling windows and crashing dishes" on Sunday evenings and Friday afternoons.

As a result, Godfrey sold the land now occupied by commercial and residential buildings. He then donated a portion of the money to an airport commission dedicated to development of a new airport. As a result, following a planning and tactical process, a new airport in its present location was completed and operational in 1964. Because of Godfrey's involvement, the airport is named Leesburg Executive Airport at Godfrey Field. He referred to it as the "Old Cow Pasture."

THE PERSON

The Donaldson family at the time lived near the Godfrey property in Paeonian Springs. The son, Bruce Donaldson, who was seven years old at the time, remembers Godfrey, whom his mom and dad knew quite well. Bruce said, "Godfrey used to buzz their house to let his wife, Mary, know to come and pick him up at the airport." He remembers, too, that he saw Godfrey riding his horse Goldie in their yard. And he said his mom sang in a choir with Mary Godfrey.

Bruce remembers Godfrey as having a somewhat gruff exterior. But once you got beyond that, he was friendly. Bruce's dad liked organic farming and wanted to do some plantings on one part of their land. Godfrey was kind enough to "send him seeds" for that purpose. He was known as something of an environmentalist and at one point had elk and bison on his land. And Bruce said that he also had an elephant for a time. He did like hunting and went on safari to Africa on several occasions.

Eeda Dennis, who lived with her husband, Alfred, in Leesburg back then, said she met him once with her mother-in-law and remembers him as being "pleasant. We talked about the weather."

Godfrey received a number of awards, including induction into the National Association of Broadcasters Hall of Fame, Peabody Award, Hollywood Walk of Fame and Meritorious Service to Aviation Award.

Arthur Godfrey died in 1983 at the age of seventy-nine. Despite his heritage in New York, he found his home in Leesburg, where he is buried in the Union Cemetery.

Published in *Reflections* magazine

Chapter 12

GERALDINE BROOKS

2008

Geraldine Brooks stood at the podium at the National Press Club talking to a filled audience about her latest book, titled *People of the Book*. She spoke in soft but legible tones, heavy with an Aussie accent—a product of her heritage. Her round face and neat, short cropped hair framed lively brown eyes and a ready smile. *People of the Book*, a novel, describes the odyssey of a fifteenth-century Haggadah—a book containing the liturgy for the Seder service in the Jewish festival of Passover. This one also contains colorful illustrations that give it special significance in addition to its age, and it debunks the idea that medieval Hebrew books deliberately exclude such art.

The novel traces the Haggadah on a hazardous road of survival from Seville to Tarragona to Venice and finally to Sarajevo, where it now resides in a museum. It is known as the Sarajevo Haggadah. Her novel spent several weeks on the *New York Times* bestseller list and on the *Washington Post* Book World list.

I asked her how she got the idea for *People of the Book*. She replied, "Ernest Hemingway once said that the best way to get ideas for stories is in bars. I overheard someone talking about the Haggadah in a bar in Sarajevo."

While *People* is her latest literary offering, she has several others to her credit, including the 2006 Pulitzer Prize–winning *March*. When I read that, I was taken by how well she could put the reader into that period, during the American Civil War. I thought it quite fascinating that someone from Australia could create so clearly a nineteenth-century American environment.

Geraldine Brooks. *Photo by Randi Baird.*

She said, "I have Tony [her husband, Tony Horwitz] to thank for a pretty thorough education by osmosis—being dragged sometimes kicking and screaming to endless reenactments and battlefield tours and even horse burials at VMI while he was researching *Confederates in the Attic.*"

She continued her explanation: "I was lucky to come across an amazing memoir by a man named Knox who'd been a Yankee carpetbagger." The New England aspects she says she got from Bronson Alcott's journals and letters. "I have deep U.S. roots. My father's family were in this country since 1630 and lived in New England until the 1900s."

Horwitz, the author of *Confederates*, won a Pulitzer for his journalistic skills, reporting nationally. Geraldine said, "We met in Columbia Journalism School. We fell for each other in Karen Rothmyer's business reporting class—two lefties trying to figure out how to cover the capitalists." They married in Tourrettes-sur-Loup, France, in 1984.

Brooks, who grew up in the western suburbs of Sydney, reached her destination as a novelist by way of journalism. "I wanted to be a newspaper reporter from the time I was eight and visited the newspaper where my dad worked as a proofreader. The thunder of rolling presses, the sense of being first to know the news of my city—I was hooked from that day."

She attended Bethlehem College Ashfield and the University of Sydney. She went on to be a reporter for the *Sydney Morning Herald* and later a feature writer whose interest grew into environmental issues. After a stint at Columbia University as a journalism graduate student, she joined the staff at the *Wall Street Journal* and became one of their foreign correspondents. That took her not only a long way from her recent home in Waterford but also into battle zones in the Balkans and Iraq after the First Gulf War.

Her most harrowing experience? Covering the collapse of the Kurdish uprising. Right after the First Gulf War, President Bush allowed Saddam Hussein to use helicopter gunships that flew north to the Kurdish regions, where an uprising was in progress, and they started strafing civilians. She said, "Kurds fled for the borders by the thousands, and we journalists went with them. I hiked over the mountains to refuge in Turkey, but a young colleague, a photographer named Gad Gross, was shot by Iraqi forces."

Brooks and Horwitz, along with their family of a son and three dogs, lived in Waterford, Virginia, for ten years before moving to Martha's Vineyard three years ago. Her hobbies include reading, which she says is "huge," and gardening; she has a "large summer organic veggie parterre and a number of flower borders." She says she loves to cook, "especially big, robust ethnic dishes like gumbo and tagines and curry of all kinds."

She likes taking her three dogs on "long, exploratory rambles in the woods and along waterways." She says she has taken up the cello, which "has the family wincing a lot."

She starts her day with an hour of exercise as the sun first peeks over the horizon—she says, "otherwise, it doesn't get done." After preparing breakfast and school lunches, she goes to work when her son leaves for school. She stays with it until he gets home. Then she tends the garden and cooks and says, "It's amazing how many plot points can get resolved while you're kneading bread or turning compost."

I asked her about the differences between journalism and book writing. "Simply, it holds that news stories, magazine stories can't go beyond 'provable facts,' while novels give the writer the license to do so. She said, "Fiction can and must do so."

Likely never to return to journalism, she is plugging away on another historical novel that takes place in New England in 1666, which she says is one of her favorite years.

As she began to conclude her presentation at the Press Club, she said, "Someone once asked Leon de Modena, a seventeenth-century Venetian rabbi, what made a good sermon. He said, 'Tell them it's forty minutes and make it twenty, or tell them it's twenty and make it ten.' That's why his sermons were so widely praised." Certainly, the same kind of praise could apply to Brooks. She went on and patiently answered questions from her audience—an audience that gave her an enthusiastic ovation, to which she gracefully responded before proceeding to meet members of her audience personally, chatting and signing their copies of *People of the Book*.

In 2022, Brooks wrote a book titled *Horse* that sat at the top of the *New York Times* bestseller list.

Published in *elan* magazine

Chapter 13

EEDA DENNIS

2020

Eeda Dennis, longtime resident of Leesburg, can be considered a matriarch of Leesburg and Loudoun County. I asked her what she liked about Loudoun County, and she said, "Except for the heat in the summer, the climate, the trees, gardens, the people—I just like everything about Loudoun County."

Dennis grew up in Norway and said she enjoyed skiing and her family life there. When she was a teenager, she and her family endured the Nazi occupation from 1940 to 1945. Her father was in the resistance. "Everyone was. Our family had life's essentials, and the Nazis took everything. We no longer had food." According to an interview she had with Cheryl Sadowski for a book titled *Afternoons with Eeda*, she estimated that 80 percent of Norwegians were opposed to the Nazis. She used to go around with what appeared to be a copy of Hitler's book *Mein Kampf* under her arm when she went to school. "I wrapped the cover around an English textbook to hide the fact I was studying English. The Nazis didn't allow that."

She met her husband, Alfred Dennis, in Norway, where he was stationed as a member of the U.S. Foreign Service. She explained that she met him at a going-away party her dad had set up for her before she left for Paris to attend college. After getting married, they moved to Sage Hill Farm, into Alfred's mother's home that was built in 1938. Sage Hill is in Leesburg, on Edwards Ferry Road. They were in and out given Alfred's job—assignments in Naples, Italy; Africa; and Iceland. Finally, after retirement, they settled at Sage Hill. Alfred passed away in 2009.

NORTHERN VIRGINIA LUMINARIES

Eeda has served on the George C. Marshall Center board since its inception. She said that her dad told her if it hadn't been for the Marshall Plan following World War II, they would have starved and been taken over by the Russians. Marshall lived in Leesburg for twelve years in Dodona Manor along Edwards Ferry Road. Eeda recalled driving with her mother-in-law one day when "we saw this man out painting the entrance to his house. My mother-in-law said, 'That's General Marshall; let's stop and say hello.'" She said he had paint on his face. Eeda was awestruck—"This is the man who saved us?"

She lavished praise on an active preservationist, Mr. B. Powell Harrison, for keeping Marshall's house and property from being turned into a shopping center. He was able to convene several prominent Leesburg citizens who raised money to buy the home and some surrounding property in the early 1990s with the George C. Marshall Home Preservation Fund. It is now the George C. Marshall Center, and to this day, it's a museum. Out of respect for Marshall, Eeda has continued her service on the board all these years.

Another passion of hers is gardening. She has membership in the Leesburg Garden Club and was asked to be president, but about that time, her father was fatally ill in Norway, and she had to take trips to her old hometown. She did later take the job as program chairperson, giving talks and setting up events.

Eeda Dennis. *Photo by Rene Dennis.*

Because of being so much a part of the county, the Dennises know and have known many of the prominent people in Loudoun: Ms. A.V. Symington; Russell Baker; Ms. Vinton Pickens, who was responsible for there being no billboards in the county; Mrs. Marshall and her daughter and son-in-law; Mr. and Mrs. Winn; former Leesburg mayor Bob Sevila; Keith Wauchope, former ambassador to Gabon; and Jean and Joseph Pendergast, owners of James Monroe's home, Oak Hill, south of Leesburg.

Sage Hill has remained rural and has some attachment to history. For example, there are Civil War trenches on the property along Edwards Ferry Road. Alfred once said that they had found Confederate and Union artifacts such as belt buckles and buttons from uniforms. Of course, Edwards Ferry Road is historic in itself. It's where Union troops marched down to the Potomac River to cross on their way to Gettysburg. The Dennis home sits on high ground, built from brown stone with a view of the Potomac; Harrison Island, occupied at one time by Indians; and Sugarloaf Mountain. Alfred once said that during the Second World War, there was a demand for sage. Responding to that, his mother raised sage on her farm, hence the name Sage Hill. Eeda remains comfortably in her home.

Eeda and Alfred have three sons and four grandsons. She remains committed to preservation and gardening.

Chapter 14

GEORGE C. MARSHALL

2010

D ocents, board members or contributors of the George C. Marshall International Center (GCMIC) have included Tom Flynn, Ann Horstman, Bonita Metz, Richard Van Antwerp and Laurie Makamodo, along with many others. Dr. Edgar Hatrick served as the GCMIC board chairperson. He had been a member of the board since 1995 and was formerly the Loudoun County school superintendent.

General Marshall and his wife, Katherine Tupper Marshall, lived in Dodona Manor from 1941 to 1953, and during that period, he was army chief of staff, secretary of state, secretary of defense and president of the American Red Cross. In 1953, he was the recipient of the Nobel Peace Prize for the European recovery plan that bears his name. During these war years and his service to his country and indeed to the world, he also had a private life. The Marshalls have five grandchildren who spent time with him at their home. Three of them visited there within the last five years and discussed their relationship with the general.

Kitty Winn is an actress and drew her fondness for the stage from her mother. She commented, "When she married George Marshall, she was on the world stage."

Her sister Eileen described General Marshall's personality as she knew it: "I never saw him upset, and he had a good sense of humor." The family referred to him as Colonel—even after he became a general—because he was a Colonel when he married Katherine. Eileen said that as grandchildren, they called him "Undaddy" after her brother Jim Winn, who was trying to say "granddaddy."

Jim Winn, an attorney from Baltimore, said his grandfather enjoyed horseback riding, canoeing, hunting, fishing and gardening. "Once after he started planting corn, he gave me an ear to plant. So I dug a hole in the ground and stuck the ear in. Undaddy laughed and showed me how to shave off the kernels and plant them."

He remembered that his grandfather gave him his first sport coat, shared his dogs with him and took him and his sisters to the circus.

Meanwhile, General Marshall was tending to business. He organized and directed the resources for America in the Second World War, and later, with the implementation of the Marshall Plan, he became a household name in Europe.

George C. Marshall. *Courtesy of the Library of Congress.*

His speech at Harvard on June 5, 1947, which proposed the European recovery program, was made without consultation with President Truman. I was told by Marshall scholar Rachel Thompson that he did this so that the president wouldn't be blamed if it went awry. With all that Marshall had done in the war effort and as a common-sense advisor to both Roosevelt and Truman, this was his paramount moment in history.

Winston Churchill called Marshall "the noblest Roman of them all."

The newly restored home of General George C. Marshall, Dodona Manor in Leesburg, had its opening to the public in the fall of 2005. While the interior of the home gives one the impression of being in the 1940s and 1950s, when the Marshalls lived there, the George C. Marshall International Center continues to collect and appoint the home to further fulfill its goal of historic and cultural authenticity. The center sponsors events and conducts educational and exchange programs designed to illuminate and continue the legacy of Marshall.

General Marshall, being a career military man, had Spartan living quarters: a twin bed, chair, nightstand and dresser. It reminded me of an army barracks. One of his only concessions to décor was a carpet bearing his name in Chinese, a gift from Madame Chiang Kai-shek, an occasional guest of the Marshalls. By contrast, the guest room is bright and spacious, with a fireplace and relatively lavish furnishings. It seemed to me that in some ways it portrayed his worldview. As a matter of course, he never asked anything for himself yet authored a plan that rebuilt Europe after World War II.

Dodona Manor, the Marshall Home. *Courtesy of the Marshall International Center.*

Dodona Manor was built in the early 1800s on 8.0 acres of land. When the Marshalls bought the property, it was 3.8 acres, the same parcel that you see today in the town of Leesburg between East Market Street and Edwards Ferry Road. Upon returning from a trip abroad in 1942, Marshall said, "This is home…a real home after forty-one years of wandering."

There have been as many as forty-five docents who conduct tours of the manor. Rachel Thomson has been instrumental in formulating a training program for the docents, who are well versed in the Marshall legacy. Her book, titled *Marshall: A Statesman in the Crucible of War*, reflects her scholarly knowledge of General Marshall.

Rachel says she relied on Dr. William Seale, an eminent architectural historian and author of the book *The President's House*, for source material, such as interpretation of the house, and archival materials including interviews with friends and relatives who knew the Marshalls when they lived at Dodona.

What one historian described as the "greatest American since George Washington" lived in Leesburg, juggling his global commitments with gardening and with his grandchildren.

One story that touches an emotional chord concerns his assignment by President Eisenhower to attend the coronation of Queen Elizabeth in June 1953. He entered Westminster Abbey accompanied by General Omar Bradley. At that moment, the entire congregation stood, whereupon Marshall whispered to Bradley, "What are they standing for?"

Bradley replied, "They are standing for you."

Chapter 15

ROGER MUDD

2009

Roger Mudd sat comfortably in his 1860s vintage home in McLean, recognizable as the Roger Mudd of television and radio fame. At age eighty-one, only his hair has given up its dark tint to gray, and his sideburns—the style of his heyday—no longer exist. His era was the '60s, '70s and '80s, when television news was at its peak, as he describes in his recently published book, *The Place to Be*. He wrote, "There were 50, 60, or 100 came through the CBS Bureau in 20 years. I got most of them and they were delighted to be asked to talk about it because they were proud of what they had done." Roger goes on to say that the book "tries by indirection—that is critical of today's television without being critical. It tries to show the way television used to be. And it isn't anymore."

In those years, Mudd was weekend anchor for CBS, co-anchor of *NBC Nightly News* and co-host of NBC's *Meet the Press*. He received five Emmys for his work, as well as the Peabody Award and the John Shorenstein Award for distinguished Washington reporting. His name was synonymous with valid, unadulterated, straightforward news reporting. He is a charter member of that pantheon of giants in the news industry: Walter Cronkite, Daniel Schorr, Dan Rather, Marvin Kalb, Eric Sevareid.

He came to his interest and his career in journalism somewhat obliquely. He was in graduate school in North Carolina, majoring in history. His thesis was titled "Roosevelt and the Press." As he said, "I had a lot of fun with it. My sources were newspapers and the Library of Congress." For his research, he chose several newspapers that covered the political landscape from left to right. He had been encouraged to get a PhD. "But before I did, I thought I should really go to work for a newspaper and find out how it worked."

He got a job with the *Richmond News Leader* in 1953. From there, he crossed the street and joined the *News Leader*–owned radio station, and then in 1956, "I came up here—this is my home—and worked for channel 9, 1956 to 1961." And then Howard K. Smith hired him at CBS. Those were the banner years that took him through historic events such as Robert Kennedy's assassination; the civil

Roger Mudd, McLean, Virginia.
Photo by Woody Wrable.

rights filibuster in the Senate in 1964; a documentary with Ted Kennedy; and pinch hitting for Walter Cronkite during summer months in the '70s and '80s.

His most memorable experience? He said, "Probably the first one I remember, the first big one, was when I was assigned to anchor the CBS coverage of the march on Washington in 1963. This was the Martin Luther King 'I Have a Dream' speech."

For one thing, he said, the federal government was terrified, not knowing what was going to happen. "They ordered all the bars in Washington closed, and they got the Washington Senators baseball team to postpone their game. They were afraid that there would be racial violence. But nothing happened. Nothing happened at all."

He was on the steps of the Lincoln Memorial near one of the parapets with a card table and chairs. "I had kind of big airline pilot headphones on. Big, big mikes." It was to be a live broadcast. "And you're not reading on the teleprompter, and you don't know what's going to happen. Your career's on the line."

He said he got there about 9:15 for a 10:00 a.m. broadcast. "I didn't feel very well. It got worse and worse, and I started taking deep breaths and chewing Tums and drinking Cokes, and I went down behind the boxwood and threw up. I was okay after that."

I asked Mudd what interesting characters he encountered during his career. He cited the southern senators, especially Richard Russell of Georgia. He said, "They tell better stories, more outrageous. They are

NORTHERN VIRGINIA LUMINARIES

funnier. They drink a little more than others." And Russell, he said, was a man of respect and bearing (despite his racial views) and "was an absolute master of Senate procedure."

Roger got a deep insight into the workings of the Senate when he covered the civil rights filibuster that lasted for sixty-four days. "It's the first time a civil rights filibuster had been broken."

We talked about the newscasters he respects the most: "Walter Cronkite and Jim Lehrer because they both regarded the news as a precious commodity to be handled with care."

And journalism today? He shifted in his chair and with no hesitation said, "You don't recognize it today. It's so different from my time that it's not only changes that are technical but also substantive." Deregulation, he said, under Carter and Reagan caused an explosion from the original four networks into at first twenty or thirty stations and then, later on, five hundred or so. The original three or four stations he referred to as "gatekeepers." He said, "You now have news channels that operate 24/7, so the great news organizations couldn't wait until 6:30 and do careful, considered, judicious newscasts." That, he thinks, really undermines the substance, as "the appetite for more and more stuff to fill the airways was so voracious that sort of any piddly little story got on the air."

He thinks the Internet has perhaps sounded the death knell for newspapers. According to his discussions with some of his peers, the *New York Times*—which he says provides his news—the *Washington Post* and *Los Angeles Times* may survive.

The last phase of Roger Mudd's television career was as the documentary host on the History Channel starting in the early 1990s:

> *Every Wednesday night for ten years. It was an interesting job, a rewarding job. They lost their compass about five or six years ago when they began to abandon the legitimate history documentaries and went off on series about the ice truckers and the ice highway. One of the problems was that it was so instantly popular, and the audience was large for a cable operation; they didn't feel they had to invest in a serious research department to check out whether these documentaries from out-of-house producers were really backed up by research. I could see where it was going, so in 2004, I chose not to have my contract renewed.*

To read *The Place to Be* is to take the pulse of a time in this country's history when television newscasting was at the pinnacle, with the icons of the industry issuing factual reports that met strict ethical journalism standards. In Mudd's book, he says, "For me and the hundreds of others in the Washington Bureau these 20 years were the glory years of television news." The book, he says, is a memoir, but it is mostly the story of the men and women who served in the great CBS Washington Bureau. For more than two decades, they will tell you—it was the place to be.

Published in *elan* magazine
At age ninety-one, Roger Mudd lived in McLean and occasionally could be seen on the History Channel. He passed away late in 2021.

Chapter 16

GARY POWERS JR.

2007

I met Francis Gary Powers Jr. in the lobby of the Marriott Hotel at Dulles Airport. He had just come up on business from Richmond, where he now lives. His business? The creation and development of a Cold War museum.

Gary, with a round face, a ready smile and animated dark eyes, resembled photos of his dad, the former U-2 pilot who caused a stir when his spy plane was shot down over the Soviet Union on May 1, 1960. Gary Powers Sr. was a U.S. Air Force pilot and then flew spy planes for the CIA. This day, he was flying a standard run at 70,500 feet, nearing the city of Sverdlovsk in the former Soviet Union, when his plane was struck by a ground-to-air missile. He eventually bailed out as the plane began to disintegrate while plummeting toward the ground.

The incident brought the United States and the Soviet Union close to confrontation during the Cold War. According to reports, the senior Powers endured "61 days of rigorous interrogation followed by a conviction for espionage" that carried with it a ten-year sentence.

Almost two years later, Powers was exchanged for a Soviet spy, Colonel Rudolf Abel, on February 10, 1962, in a dramatic scene at the so-called Bridge of Spies, the Glienicke Bridge in Potsdam, Germany. Powers later became a helicopter traffic reporter in Los Angeles.

Gary Jr. had not been born yet when all this occurred, but his memories of his dad and that experience remain. "I remember my father as a normal dad who was a pilot. I would fly with him in the afternoons and in the mornings before school when he was doing the air traffic reporting for the local radio station (KGIL)."

Gary Powers Jr. *Photo by Gary Powers.*

Gary said they used to go hiking and biking, and his dad took him fishing. "I just thought it was a normal childhood. I was aware that he had been shot down, imprisoned and exchanged for a Soviet spy. We talked about it. I thought it was normal. I thought everybody's dad had been through this. That perception changed on August 1, 1977, when he died in the helicopter crash."

From the feature story in *Reader's Digest* in 2003:

> *On August 1, 1977, at 12:38 PM, Francis Gary Powers died when the helicopter he was piloting crashed with an empty gas tank into an open field in Encino, California....Had a system malfunction caused the gas gauge to read empty or had Powers simply tried to push the helicopter beyond its limits in an attempt to return to base not too far away? As the last drop of fuel was being used up, Powers made a quick maneuver to avoid some children who had suddenly appeared beneath him. There is a belief that this maneuver prevented him from making a safe landing.*

Gary Jr. said that the helicopter was headed for a baseball field with kids playing ball when his dad swerved to avoid them. "My dad had said that the gas gauge on the helicopter was faulty. He had learned that there was still twenty minutes of flying time remaining when the gauge read empty. We think that when the helicopter went in for servicing, the service people fixed the gauge and didn't tell Dad."

It was after that tragic event that Gary says he became more aware of Cold War history and his dad's involvement in it. "By the time I realized the significance of it, it was too late to ask any questions." Gary was twelve years old when his dad's helicopter went down.

He remembered talking with his dad about his experience in Russia. "He would share some memories of what it was like to bail out of a plane. I remember talking to him about the jail cell, what he was doing inside and the interrogations—some really good memories about that."

Francis Gary Powers, U-2 pilot. *Courtesy of the Cold War Museum.*

Gary Jr. said he always used to ask his dad how high he was flying. Night after night, the same question. One evening, he said, "Dad, how high were you flying?"

"Gary," his dad said, "not high enough! Now go to bed."

Apparently, his father's experience planted a seed in young Gary that germinated through the years and eventually resulted in his founding the Cold War Museum in 1996—"to honor Cold War Veterans and preserve Cold War history."

He began to think seriously about the Cold War when he attended college at California State University–Northridge. He said he was motivated by the trauma of his dad's death and widespread recognition of what his dad had been through. "In college, I realized I had better know as much as possible. I had better know how to answer questions, and they had better be factually correct."

He began to do research. "I had to know more about the U-2 incident. And from that, I had to understand the Cold War to better understand my father."

He was further spurred when he spoke to students about that incident and got, as he says, "blank stares. They thought I was there to talk about the U-2 rock band." That, he says, "was the light bulb—something had to be done to preserve Cold War history."

Gary said the museum—which at the moment is on standby waiting to occupy the former Lorton Prison in Lorton, Virginia—has over $3 million worth of artifacts, including the U-2 helmet worn by Francis Gary Powers, wreckage from the U-2 plane, an East German Trabant (a twenty-eight-horsepower car), a nuclear attack survival kit and a vast array of other items depicting an era that had everyone on alert. In those days, private residents built bomb shelters and stored food in case of a Russian-instigated nuclear attack. Paranoia gripped the country. The Cuban Missile Crisis, the Bay of Pigs and the Polish and Hungarian uprisings all occurred during the Cold War and will be part of the new museum.

Gary said that his organization will have twenty-six acres on the former Lorton Prison grounds and that each of the buildings will represent a decade during the Cold War—from the 1940s into the 1990s. Funding has come from the State of Virginia and private sources. He is the director of the museum and the only paid person; the board members and others are volunteers.

A mobile exhibit specifically about the U-2 incident went on the road this past September. The museum has been collaborating with the International Spy Museum in Washington and the Atomic Bunker in Harnekop near Berlin to exhibit some of its artifacts. The Cold War Museum has an

Francis Gary Powers and son Gary Powers Jr. *Courtesy of the archives of Knox News.*

affiliation with the Smithsonian Air and Space, American History, National Portrait and U.S. Postal Museums.

Gary comes by his position naturally. He graduated in 1990 from California State University in Los Angeles with a degree in philosophy. Then in 1995, he received a master's degree in public administration with a certification in nonprofit management from George Mason University in Fairfax, Virginia. In 2002, he was selected by the Junior Chamber of Commerce as one of Ten Outstanding Young Americans. He lectures internationally and has been a regular on the History, Discovery and A&E Channels.

His father initially was pilloried for, of all things, failing to die by suicide rather than be captured by the Soviets. In later years, he was given the recognition he deserved for his service to his country. In May 2000 at Beale Air Force Base in California, in a ceremony attended by Gary, his mother, Sue; and his sister, Dee, Francis Gary Powers was posthumously awarded the Distinguished Flying Cross, the POW Medal and the Central Intelligence Agency Director's Award. On that same day, the U.S. Air Force seated Gary in the back of a U-2 trainer that took him to an altitude of seventy-three thousand feet.

Gary is married with one son, whose name is Francis Gary Powers III. Gary's reverence for his father has been passed along.

And now the Cold War Museum has become a reality after being initiated in 1996. It is located near Warrenton, Virginia, and has relics from the Cold War. Its location has additional historical significance, as it is on turf that during World War II was an army camp appropriately situated on ground where German and Japanese messages could be intercepted.

Gary Powers Jr. is active as a writer, journalist and historian. He has two books out: *Letters from a Soviet Prison* (2017) and *Spy Pilot* (2019). He serves on several boards and organizations involving Cold War history, aerospace, the International Spy Museum, the National Park Service and more. He was a consultant for Steven Spielberg in making the movie *Bridge of Spies* about the prisoner exchange in Germany when his father was released from prison in Russia.

Published in *Grapevine* magazine

Chapter 17

DAVID KAY

2004

D avid Kay and his wife, Anita, lived in an environ of Leesburg. David looks more like a soft-spoken professor—as he was in a past life—in an Ivy League school, rather than the high-profile chief weapons inspector in Iraq, who has held the world stage for several weeks. Newly retired, he seems content to be home in a comfortable setting far from the war zone he just left. He and Anita's preferred tastes: to drive into the rural sections of the county and enjoy the scenery, then sample the wine at some of Loudoun's wineries. "We like Breaux Winery. I think it was last year we even went there on a weekend this time of year, and it just happened to be an unseasonably warm day. We sat out on the terrace, munched on bread and cheese and sipped wine from the Breaux Vineyard," said David.

Anita, her blondish hair neatly combed, likes the horse country and to go to Middleburg, she said, and has a penchant for the boutiques in Leesburg, the Premium Outlets and Dulles Town Center.

Before moving to Loudoun County, they lived in Reston and frequented Leesburg. "We used to dine at a restaurant called the Green Door or something like that. We now enjoy its replacement, the Eiffel Tower, and knowing its owner, Madeleine."

Their taste for French food came naturally from spending five years in Paris with UNESCO. That was followed by eight years in Vienna with the International Atomic Energy Commission, which gave David at least some of the requisite experience for his later job. After two years in London as head of a uranium trade association, he was recruited by the UN following the First Gulf War to be in charge of a team of weapons inspectors in Iraq.

He had joined the CIA for his latest assignment and had a 1,400-member staff. He said, "I had taken the job with a written guarantee that the staff level would remain untouched. But as Iraq became more dangerous than expected, the military kept pulling people away and left me short-handed. So I decided to resign. Besides, I figured we had completed about 85 percent of the process."

He said the hunt for weapons entailed following paper trails, interviewing, identifying facilities and offering rewards, which brought forward a host of storytellers—most of whom led them nowhere.

As further testimony to the danger, one civilian with Kellogg Brown and Root who recently returned from Baghdad said that he had to wear a flak jacket, typically had bodyguards even riding up the elevator in his hotel and awoke one morning as the building shook from an explosion down the street.

David's previous public statement that they had found "no large stockpiles of weapons…and they got it wrong" is widely known, causing a scramble in both the White House and the Congress and prompting President Bush to form a nine-member commission to report on what went wrong with the intelligence-gathering process. During our interview, the phone rang—one of several times—but this time, Anita called David to the phone. It was the White House telling him that the president wanted to see him immediately. He apologized, changed clothes and took off, saying later that it was the fastest he had ever gotten to Washington. "I wasn't sure how to drive myself into the White House grounds, as previously I had had a car and driver."

A theory has been posited that sometime following the First Gulf War, Saddam Hussein depleted his weapons of mass destruction but professed that he did have them to use as a bargaining chip in exchange for the international community lifting the sanctions. David said, "That's credible, and further, we know that he used these weapons before against his own people, so to maintain that political control he had to give the illusion at least that he had them. Also, he looked upon himself as the foremost Arab leader—patterned after Saladin—and as such could not be seen knuckling under to U.S. pressure."

Some Arabists say that Iraq, with its factions, religious and otherwise, is ripe for a civil war. David says, "I think that could well be and maybe with more than two sides. You have a split among the Shia, then you have the Sunnis and, of course, the Kurds in the north."

His future is unsettled at the moment. He knows only that they will remain in Loudoun County. David says he will take his time to sort out the many job offers that have come his way. Anita mentioned the Potomac Institute, a think tank, as a possibility. She, of course, is happy to have him back safely. "I watched far too much television while he was gone, and every time we'd hear about a bombing, I grew fearful. But he phoned once or twice a day so that I'd know he was okay."

From war zone to Loudoun County. Both Anita and David seem happy with that transition.

2006

Most people know David Kay and his reputation as the former chief weapons inspector in Iraq. Now, an increasing number are becoming acquainted with his photography.

He says, "I started photography when our daughter was born in 1966. I wanted to document it."

Then, after he came to Washington, he had friends who worked for *National Geographic*, and his interest in photography began to grow. "And I started to do more serious photography." He credits Dick Durrance and Bob Krist, both travel photographers, and Brenda Tharp, whose specialty is nature and travel photography, with giving him added incentive and training in the art of photography.

He says that about the same time, he was able to do "performance photography." "I got to know ballet dancers around town and took photos of the ballet at Wolf Trap." Then, as he puts it, "we picked up our bags and moved to Europe." That gave him an opportunity to do some travel photography in Paris and Vienna, among his favorite spots.

In 1990, his first tour in Iraq interrupted his photographic career. "I put down my camera and didn't pick it up again until the beginning of 2004."

He says he has been influenced to an extent by documentaries, and his photography over the years has evolved, as has his philosophy of photographing. "I have an objective. I think the best photographs tell stories. If they don't tell stories, then they should let the viewers tell a story of their own." He goes on to say that in his opinion, a photo should draw whoever looks at it into it rather than its being just an object. He likes to look at other photos to see what "works and, quite frankly, what doesn't work."

While he was in Europe, his travel photography almost always involved people. He says, "The law is different than in the United States. In Europe,

David Kay. *Photo from David Kay.*

you can photograph people and publish it without getting written permission. In the States, you have to get permission."

He has an agent who takes his photographs and has them published. Generally, he doesn't have a clue where. But one time, he says he was on a flight and pulled out the airline magazine from the pouch in the back of the seat, and there were three of his photos. He's published in textbooks and magazines, and he says, "I got a picture of spinach in a market out in California. The most ordinary subject—just a bunch of leafy spinach. It sells almost every week. The only thing we can figure is that it's some grocery store flyer advertising specials."

One of his favorite places to photograph is the Leesburg Farmers' Market off Catoctin Circle. He says he likes to go there around 8:00 a.m., before they open at 9:00. "The people are nice and accommodating." And although he sometimes gets flak from his wife, Anita, he likes to take photos of the food they eat at restaurants. He showed me one of a martini—a close-up looking straight down, the circular rim of the glass and the glass itself covering the entire frame; balloon-like olives; cool, refreshing liquid with frosty droplets on the glass. "An ideal situation: I took photos of it then got to drink it." Another one, a plate of oysters, had texture, random shapes and depth.

He has four six-megapixel digital cameras, all Nikons: a D2, D100, 70 and 200. "One of the great things about digital photography is that you can see right away what you shoot." He uses a combination of shutter opening and speed to make a tradeoff between light and depth of field. He rarely modifies or enhances his photos once he downloads them to the computer. "I would rather spend my time with a camera than in front of a computer."

He advocates photographing early in the morning. "Photography is really painting with light, and the light is most suitable early in the morning up until about 10:00 a.m., unless the day is overcast."

A prime example of early morning photography is his photo of an American flag with a fog-shrouded tall ship in the background. "I woke up this one morning in Maine when nothing moved. The light was exquisite." This photo struck me as one the viewer could interpret in a variety of ways—the tall ship in the midst of the fog, perhaps connoting time, could represent the nation's past; the flag in the foreground the present; the two connected and depending on your viewpoint; the motionless flag could have several meanings.

He has a penchant for bright colored flowers—roses, irises, tulips and sunflowers—and sharply contrasting hues. He admits to preferring reds, as evident in several photos of roses. He occasionally does something involving multiple exposures overlaying each other, in which the photo produces a gauze-like image along with a blurry impression of movement. A green frog peers enigmatically in another he took at his fishpond in Bethany, Maryland. As if to define himself with topical diversity, he showed me another of his favorites: silhouetted fishermen on the beach. One of a dock on the coast of Maine had color with a splendid sunrise and fascinating geometric patterns within a tangle of pilings and piers. Still another of a tidal pool with "the sun just right" and given combinations of shutter speed, exposure settings and time-lapse photography, he has created the appearance of flowing quicksilver.

But likely his overall favorite, he says, is a photograph of an elderly woman's hands taken during a holiday in Belgium. "This is really the kind of stuff I like to do. You can read experience, integrity, whatever you want into these hands."

Photographic locales and subjects range all over the world. He had one he showed me of a rack of bras across the front of a shop in Tuscany. "I try to illustrate concepts, balance and challenge." He has photos of sculptures in the New York Museum of Modern Art; a bunch of purple grapes with contrasting green leaves taken at Hillsboro Vineyard; a camel head in a market in Marrakesh; and kiteboarders off the Eastern Seaboard.

It seems fairly obvious that David Kay, who has been consistently in the news with regard to his "other" profession as a chief weapons inspector, has cast off that mantle in favor of perhaps a less dangerous, more artistic endeavor. It's equally obvious that he prefers that to seeking WMD.

Published in *Loudoun Times Mirror* and *elan* magazine
David Kay died in 2022.

Chapter 18

CHARLIE DAVIS

2006

On a bright sunny day at eleven o'clock in the morning, a hulk of a man with a long beard came up to him. "Amerikanski?" He repeated this three times while Charles had his hand on his sidearm, a cocked .45 tucked under his jacket. "Finally, I said yes. Then the man, whom he later learned was Mr. Slavko Jevtovic, came up to me and kissed me three times on first one cheek and then the other. That's the tradition of the Eastern Orthodox—for Father, Son and Holy Ghost."

Charles Davis, a dapper eighty-nine-year-old, can recall in great detail his experiences in World War II. He was a bombardier/navigator as part of the 459th Bombardment Group in the 15th Air Force aboard a B-24 shot down over Yugoslavia on their fourteenth bombing mission. He and his fellow crew members eluded capture by the Germans, thanks to General Mihailovich and his resistance fighters after they bailed out over Serbia.

The plane took off from Giulia Field in Italy on June 6, 1944, with the objective of hitting fuel tanks in Romania. "The primary target was clouded over," said Charles, "so we went after the secondary target, a rail line leading away from the tanks. Our No. 1 engine malfunctioned; then the No. 3 engine began leaking oil." They had to break formation at that point, said Charles, when the No. 4 engine was hit.

They had been told not to abandon ship over Romania, which was hostile to Americans, so they managed to stay in the air "until we crossed the Blue Danube, which was really brown. Then we knew we were in Serbia."

Charlie Davis. *Photo from Air Force Escape and Evasion Society.*

The six-man crew parachuted onto the side of Ravna Gora (Ravna Mountain). Charles said, "As I was coming down, I could hear voices in the trees below. I didn't know whether they were friendly." As it turned out, he concentrated so much on those voices that he landed on one leg and broke his ankle. "Another of the crew also broke his ankle landing."

That's when he met Jevtovic. They carried him to where he could mount a horse, and the group proceeded to "the safety of a beautiful house with a thatched roof. The woman of the house greeted me with a small bottle. It looked like white wine. She offered it to me, and I said no at first. She took a sip then handed me the bottle. I took a big gulp and turned red and green, and my eyes watered. It was homemade plum brandy—*slivovitz*." Everyone laughed. Welcome to Serbia.

"They put me in bed and later a larger bed. The woman of the house placed a lantern on the headboard then brought me a comic book about the thickness of a *Reader's Digest*. It was an American comic book."

On June 9 or 10, Charles said, the woman came to his bedroom and said, "Davis, your birthday?" "Yes, ma'am," I replied. His twenty-fifth birthday fell on June 8. She later brought him a small cake. "How she found sugar and other ingredients I'll never know. The Germans had taken everything of value. They had been German occupied for over two years."

The whole crew moved each day from one house to another. "The people where we stayed gave us their beds while they slept on the ground or in a haystack. Food was scarce, but we had black bread and goat milk cheese in the morning and in the evening. *Slivovitz* was plentiful."

Each of the crew members had been supplied with a survival kit, Charles said. It included a map on silk to keep the colors from running in case it got wet, fishhook and string, a compass, a book and a vial of morphine. Since Charles had to have his ankle reset, the morphine came in handy. The Serbs located a man who had attended to the animals—no doctors were available. He worked on the ankle and then fashioned a splint and made a crutch. It was important that Charles be able to walk because they moved the crew to a different home each day, and walking was the chief means of transport.

Later, Charles persuaded his pilot who had been an enlisted man in the Medical Corps to try to reset the ankle, as he said, "I knew it wasn't quite right." Charles passed out during the resetting but said, "Once we returned to the States and I went to a doctor, the doctor said it was perfect and wanted to know if another physician had set the ankle. Pilot Joseph Buchler had done a perfect job."

He says the daily routine involved their staying in the house while the host family went to the fields during the day. When they came home in the late afternoon, they had dinner with whatever was available. Of course, *slivovitz* was always on hand. This went on for sixty-six days.

Charles said:

> *One time, we were being transported in an oxen-drawn wagon filled with hay. The Germans had taken virtually everything such as tractors, cars, trucks and they had hauled off farm animals except for the oxen, which were too slow and big to move. We heard the sound of something mechanized and knew it had to be Germans. Our driver pulled the wagon off the road and down to a stream for the oxen to have a drink. We covered ourselves with hay. The Germans drove by on the road and paid us little attention, as oxen drinking from a stream hitched to a wagon was a typical scene.*

Their odyssey took them to the area in Serbia near the towns of Cacak, Ivanjica and Gornji Milanovac, all of which lie south of Belgrade.

General Mihailovich's partisans, the CETNIK soldiers, were able to extract the radio from a fallen B-24. Charles said they hooked it up to the magneto on a motorcycle to recharge the radio's battery and began sending out messages. Ultimately, the OSS—the predecessor of the CIA—responded. But the OSS didn't know who was sending the messages and asked them to identify themselves. They did so by citing that one member of their crew always wore a yellow kerchief around his neck and another one had made a drawing on the inside of a tent where they were billeted in Italy. "We sent out everyone's serial numbers—enlisted men had eight digits, officers seven. Only the radioman used nine digits for eight of the enlisted men to denote the coordinates of where we were located."

One thing led to another, and eventually, the OSS created the Halyard Mission to rescue the MIA airmen. On August 10, 1944, they arranged to have seventeen C-47s land at night on a secret airstrip that General Mihailovich's troops had built. The troops had dug trenches along the sides of the dirt runway, filled them with brush and then used residual fuel from wing tip fuel tanks that had been collected from tanks discarded by fighter escorts. "That night, 252 airmen were evacuated to Italy. General Mihailovich rescued over 500 Americans between December 1943 to December 1944."

The army assigned Charles to the radar operations school at Langley Field, Virginia, and upon completion of the course, he was retained as an instructor.

These days, Charles keeps busy doing income tax returns in keeping with his training as a financial person and, as he says tapping his head, "to keep this sharp." He has been a volunteer fireman and likes to play cards with his friends sometimes at the American Legion Hall—also, he says, a place for families and charitable programs—and he reminisces.

One of his favorites is about the time they were in training at Lackland near San Antonio, Texas, staying in pyramid tents with raised wooden floors. A Gila monster took up residence underneath the floor. Charles says their place was a mess— clothes strewn everywhere, as they had no one to keep them ship shape. One morning, the lizard came out of its home and strolled into the tent. Turning his head one way and then the other, he scanned the entire tent, then turned around and went back under the floor. Charles said, "That was when we decided we had better tidy up!" Likely the lizard and his tent mates had no idea what else life had in store for him.

Charles, a retired U.S. Air Force lieutenant colonel and a member of AARP, has been honored to receive the Purple Heart and the Air Medal. He has chaired the National Committee of American Airmen Rescued by General Mihailovich, Inc. and has worked to get a statue erected of General Mihailovich, who was executed by his rival, Marshal Josip Broz Tito of Yugoslavia. United States policy at the time favored Tito and didn't want to upset him because during the Cold War, Yugoslavia had warm-water ports coveted by the Soviet Union. So the statue has remained a dream. Charles was selected in 2005, the sixtieth anniversary of the end of the war in Europe, to commemorate what General Mihailovich did by presenting the Legion of Merit to the general's daughter, Dr. Gordina Mihailovich. He went with his daughter, Barbara. He also has a son who lives in Bakersfield, California. He stays in touch with the Jevtovic family.

Charlie says that he went into the U.S. Air Force because he disliked the horn they sounded at the Norfolk shipyard where he worked and had a deferment. He then saw his roommate come home one day in what Charlie says was a "spiffy uniform." "I decided to go to the recruitment office and join. I took the test and scored 95; 97 was passing. I pleaded with the sergeant, who said no way. Two days later, I received a letter saying they had reduced the standard to 95, and I was in!"

Published in *Grapevine* magazine
Charles Davis passed away in 2012.

Chapter 19

JERRY HARVEY

2009

Professor Harvey decided to redefine the word "cheating." He sent a letter to each of his students taking his class in the Department of Management Science at George Washington University. His thought process told him that "cheating is refusing to help another during a time of crisis." Now isn't that something, he thought. So "I sent a letter to each student saying essentially that 'you may take examinations with as many other people as you like. I frown on cheating. I go blind with rage if I catch anyone cheating. I define cheating as the failure to assist others on exams if they request it.'"

He says a copy of the letter found its way into the office of the dean, who commanded Jerry to come and meet with him. "He started screaming at me. Yelling," said Jerry. "He told me, 'Professor Harvey, can you imagine the absolute chaos that would occur if everyone started helping one another?'"

Professor Harvey laughed. There was a long pause, and the dean asked, "Did I just say what I thought I said?" Jerry replied, "I'm pretty sure you did."

Dr. Harvey had redefined cheating on the basis of his concern over something called anaclitic depression. "It's a Greek word (leaning on something or someone for emotional support), and it refers to a kind of depression that occurs when you're alienated from other people." He went on to say that it can be very destructive, even to the point of causing death, especially in infants. It can be a problem when someone gets fired from an organization not only for the person being discharged but also for the person who does the firing.

Jerry Harvey. *Photo by Joe Motheral.*

In addition to his newfound definition of cheating, he permitted his students to "sing their exam, dance it, write it." One student decided to cook an exam, and then the class ate it. A university official asked, "Where was his exam?" Jerry said, "As best I know…" Another student juggled his exam. Jerry said, "I thought he meant he was going to juggle it intellectually. He pulled out three balls from his back pocket and juggled for forty-five minutes, and at the end you knew Wilfred Bion's theory." Actually, Jerry said, this student paid his way through college by juggling for other groups. Thirteen students did a play in Lisner Auditorium called *Alice in O.D. Land.* That one included a 265-pound rabbit. Some brought their parents, some brought their kids, some brought their professors from other classes to assist on exams. Jerry said with a wry smile, "The professors were the worst. They didn't give them much help."

I spoke with Dr. George Solomon, one of Jerry's former students in graduate school. George was the rabbit in the performance of *Alice in O.D. Land.* He almost quit graduate school until he met Jerry and had him for a couple of courses. He said simply, "He rattled my cage."

Dr. Flynn Bucy, another former student and admirer of Jerry's, said, "He had a classroom style that let people learn. He was my dissertation chairman and put me through hell. But he could always see the other side of the coin, and unlike a lot of people, he lives his philosophy. He's one of a kind."

Sporting a salt-and-pepper mustache matching his head of hair, the bespectacled seventy-year-old speaks with a hint of a drawl indicative of his Texas heritage. He grew up in Austin, which he describes as "idyllic." His father was a postal clerk, and his mother worked in a department store.

He attended the University of Texas, where he got a PhD in social psychology. "I started out in accounting. I hated it, but I was good at it. I'll never forget the first exam. The first question was 'define asset.' I wrote that an asset is a very small donkey." He got a midnight call from his professor asking if he wanted him to count that answer. Jerry said, "That's my answer, and I'm sticking to it."

"It wasn't long before they recommended I seek another major. But the professor gave me credit," he added with a chuckle.

He did change majors and so began a career that has taken him to corporate offices, diverse organizations and classrooms at GWU. He's best known for his book titled *The Abilene Paradox*, which is required reading in many business schools. Without revealing too much about the "paradox," it concerns group dynamics and how one person's suggestion can lead others into something they don't really want to do. The book contains other "meditations on management," including the story of Captain Ahso, who flew his Japan Airline plane into San Francisco Bay, and how he dealt with the aftermath. Jerry said that pilots who have miscued in some way in the airline industry often use the "Captain Ahso defense."

He once applied, he says, the principle of the paradox to keep a church from going into hock by building, as he puts it, "a large Catholic church in the middle of a metaphorical Abilene." It turned out that the clergy really didn't want it; the parishioners didn't want it; but they were going to build it anyway. "The bus was on the road, and they needed to find a way to get off it."

He consults with NASA, and in making decisions, they frequently pose the question, "Are we on the road to Abilene?"

How did he come up with the idea of the Abilene Paradox?

"I was to give a speech in New York City on neurotic organizations. The speech was to be at 4:00 p.m. At 2:00 p.m., I didn't have the foggiest idea what I was going to say. I was sweating bullets. I tried to think of a neurotic organization, and it turned out to be my family. I just went in and winged it and told about the trip to Abilene" from Coleman, Texas, fifty miles away, to have lunch—an exercise in which four family members cheerfully went and later in discussion discovered that none of them really wanted to go in the first place.

The experience put him on the road to Abilene. As he describes it, "It was a lucky, outrageous, uproarious session." He decided then and there that he had better find out why that happened. From that, the book was born. He remembers, too, it was the day that Oklahoma defeated Texas in football, 47–28.

I asked Jerry's opinion about the well-known retired CEO of General Electric, Jack Welch, who was famous for his "rank 'em and yank 'em" policy, in which he had his managers fire the bottom 10 percent performers each year. Jerry said, "He was one of the most destructive people I've ever known. He had people in the organization distrustful of others and unwilling to help or cooperate for fear they might be successful and cause the helper to get yanked. What few people don't know is that he abandoned that policy after two years."

He's working on another book about estimating the potential of individuals, based on a golf outing he had one time in Austin when he went out as a single. The pro at the golf course asked if he would be willing to play golf with Mr. Porter, who turned out to be seventy-six-year-old man who had suffered a stroke, leaving him partly debilitated. Mr. Porter insisted on walking instead of riding a cart; had trouble putting the tee in the ground; carried a canvas bag with only four clubs; and hooked his left hand in his belt to keep it from shaking. When Mr. Porter spoke, he asked, "Wanna play for a dollar, Boy?"

"Well, I guess so Mr. Porter," Jerry said. "How many strokes will I have to give you?"

"Let me see you swing, Boy."

Jerry pulled out his driver and took a practice swing.

"With a swing like that, I don't need strokes," Mr. Porter replied.

So the round began, and Jerry says Mr. Porter hit the ball only 160 yards and then would chip up on the green and take one putt. "It took us three hours to play nine holes, and I shot a 42—good for me. But he beat me three up," said Jerry.

"I paid him a dollar."

He said to his partner, "Mr. Porter, much of golf is played between the ears."

"Hell, Boy, when you're in my shape, all of golf is played between the ears. And if you don't mind me saying so—you don't appear to have much potential!"

Despite that assessment by Mr. Porter, Jerry began his consulting career at age nineteen when Robert Blake—a managerial guru at the University of Texas—needed someone to roleplay with him for some corporate executives. After leaving UT, Jerry came to Washington and joined the National Training Laboratories, which he describes as the "Manhattan Project for group dynamics." He went from there to GWU.

His ties to Texas remain. He recently attended a reunion of the fiftieth anniversary of the American Legion team he played on from Austin that went to the national finals. He had the privilege of playing against Brooks Robinson—well known to Oriole fans. His aspirations for major-league baseball ended as he watched Robinson hit a ball that disappeared over the left field fence.

He said they held the reunion at a beer garden where everyone became "lubricated." And in typical Harvey fashion, he told a story on himself. He says he could claim to be a good fielder but a not-so-good hitter. In one big game, he was sitting on the bench when Williams, the team's best hitter, was next at bat. Suddenly, the coach yelled out, "Harvey, go in and hit for Williams." Jerry said, "All the people on the bench groaned. But I pulled out a bat and went out and started taking cuts, and the coach said, 'Harvey, what are you doing?' I said, 'I'm going to hit for Williams—that's what you told me.' 'No,' the coach said, 'I want you to *get* hit for Williams. If we lose this game, we have to play another one, and we need Williams.' I got hit for Williams and nearly broke my shoulder."

Dr. Jerry Harvey—getting hit for Williams aside—wistfully said, "I've been incredibly lucky. I really have. I'm not sure who the philosopher was who said, all of us have one idea. For whatever reason, God gave me the Abilene Paradox, and that's been enormously stimulating and helpful to me and for other people. They've even made a training movie of it in Hollywood with Hollywood actors."

If Jerry has been incredibly lucky by being granted the Abilene Paradox, then countless numbers of people and organizations have been incredibly lucky. Jerry has shown them when they are on the road to Abilene that they can get off the bus without pain or regret.

Published in *Grapevine* magazine
Thanks to Jack Wilson.
Jerry Harvey, who passed away in 2013, lived in McLean, Virginia, with his wife, Beth. You could find them often at the McLean Family Restaurant in a quiet booth eating dinner. Although retired from the university, he continued his consulting practice and planned to do so, he said, as long as he enjoyed it. His wife is from Coleman, Texas, where they may be tempted to go to Abilene for lunch and they know the road, but they know, too, how to get off the bus.

Chapter 20

ROBERT E. SIMON

2006

Robert E. Simon Jr. sat in his apartment on the thirteenth floor with a large picture window looking out above Lake Anne, the original development within the planned community of Reston—a town that he founded and one that bears his initials—while Erin took several photos. He asked his wife, Cheryl, to stand behind the photographer and make faces to put him in a comfortable mood. He said, "It helps me relax." He carries his ninety-one years on a trim frame with thinning hair; a broad, animated face with a neat silver goatee; and a sharp mind. Up until recently, he played tennis and rode his bicycle. He still walks on some of the fifty miles of trails he conceived as an enhancement for the town of Reston. I asked if he played golf, and he said, "I tried it and retired at age twenty-five because it took up too much time."

"I'm a generalist," he says. "I don't know anything, but I can find people that know something." He began to describe how he came to develop Reston. A broker offered the property, initially 6,750 acres, for $800,000 in cash over a ten-year, interest-free mortgage of $12 million. When Simon came down from New York to look at the area, he noted that Dulles Airport was just getting started, and as he put it, "The property was so beautiful, so well located, and the price was right."

He then developed a program, essentially a listing of items he considered important and appropriate. He says, "I put in everything I could think of to make a good life for all kinds of people—then crossed out the things that were too expensive or irrelevant." He then retained a large planning

Robert E. Simon. *Photo from Reston Town.*

firm to connect the program into a mass land-use plan. At the time, he says, he lived on Long Island on five acres, and he noted that his children, because of the spacing of the homes, had difficulty interacting with neighboring kids. "If you want kids to have a good time, you'd better not have large lots." He wanted childcare and townhouses, and he went all over the world to extract ideas. He says he did nothing that hadn't been done before; it was the collection that was unusual.

From that beginning in 1961, Reston has evolved into a community of fifty-eight thousand where they live, work and play. One thing that immediately strikes you about Reston is how well the trees have been preserved and how they have retained the open spaces of the 11.5 square miles along with the extensive urban development.

But the making of Robert E. Simon Jr. began way before Reston came into being. He grew up in Manhattan and attended good schools. He remembers with fondness Horace Mann, the Columbia University Normal School. He says the teachers were "fantastic, wonderful." As with most everything else, he has an opinion about education and is "dismayed about schools; one size fits all." He says he used to ride his scooter to school from Riverside Drive and 113th Street up Broadway to 120th Street, where the school was located. He says, "I passed lots of cars on the way." He was an editor on the school newspaper and the yearbook, and he played tennis.

He was also in the school quartet at the all-boys' upper school. He says, "I could sound like a baritone, but I could hit bass notes." He recalls the time his group was headed for a performance and passed a speakeasy: "Never been before. Everybody in the community knew about it except the police. We went in and sat at the bar and ordered a Tom Collins. I drank, and it was fine. My friend said, 'I'll have another,' and I said, 'I'll have another, too.' Then when it came time to get up, I couldn't." One friend got on each side of him, and they walked the four blocks to school. He says, "We got onto the stage, and I was really into it. I never sang better."

He went on to Harvard and sang in the Glee Club and with the Boston Symphony. He says the sixteen-man choir performed seven days a week and earned money to pay his tuition. "At Harvard, I wasn't into science particularly. I was more into art and literature." He played squash in college and majored in the history of Tudor England. He describes himself as an iconoclast by nature and did his thesis on the Duke of Northumberland, who was the son of Henry VII's tax collector. Henry VIII had the duke's father killed to please the anti-tax crowd, and the duke was written off, but Bob says, "I found out that the duke was born John Dudley and went by the title Viscount Lyle, the Earl of Warwick and the Duke of Northumberland, the first duke of non-royal blood." And he says he had access to the *Chronicle* at Harvard and used those for research and to write about the duke who had been discounted because of engineering the Lady Jane Grey plot. He graduated cum laude in 1935.

A turning point came when his father, the head of his real estate firm, died. Simon was twenty-one and biking in Scotland. Bob Jr. returned to the States and within a short time took over the firm after a showdown in a board meeting involving some malfeasance by his father's number-two man. About the same time, he became president of Carnegie Hall Inc. and held that position until 1960. His father had previously organized a group to buy it in 1925.

Simon takes pride in having converted one of the music halls at Carnegie where teachers would show off their pupils to parents and friends into what he refers to as a "debut" hall, where they would have thirteen to fifteen performances a week.

In 1943, he interrupted his business career to enlist in the army. "I was overage," he says, "but I couldn't stay out. It was inconceivable." He said he enlisted as a private and found out that "someone else decided what we ate, what we wore and when to get up.…I loved it!" The army soon promoted him to corporal, he says. "And I would wake up in the middle of the night trying to figure out some new combination of close order drill, how to get the squad to spread out in four directions and then get them back into formation." Three months later, the army sent him to Officer Candidate School (OCS). As an officer, the army assigned him to automotive school. "I didn't know anything about engines, but after two months, if my friend had any trouble with his or her car, I'd say, 'Stand back.'" Since then, he says that knowledge has disappeared, and "now I'm back to ground zero."

His next assignment was Harvard Business School, courtesy of the army. Winston Churchill once addressed his group at Harvard.

He ended up in the Quartermaster Corps, but the army sent him to JAG school, where he was the only non-lawyer. He says, "I distinguished myself right away by falling asleep during our indoctrination session."

His army career next took him to Kansas City and the quartermaster depot. Typically, he figured out a way to buy recreational equipment from the source in Racine, Wisconsin, instead of from Wilson or Spalding sporting goods, thus saving the army middleman charges. Prior to that, they had been paying Wilson, which bought from a broker that bought from an outfit in Racine. And instead of buying golf balls from the sporting goods companies, he went to the manufacturer in Pennsylvania to buy directly from the source, again saving the U.S. government money.

Then, he says, "I sent a letter through channels to Lieutenant General Sommerville recommending changes in the operations so as to provide delivery of football equipment in the fall and baseball equipment in the spring." The depot commander received a commendation for this innovative idea. But Simon said, "I had not initialed the letter with the major, my boss's initials, according to depot regulations. So he fired me, and I ended up in graves registration." There, he says, he noted that seven men were doing the work that could be done by two. Three weeks later, the army sent him to Belgium and then on to Paris, where the Quartermaster Corps serviced the troops in the European theater.

It takes only a couple hours with Robert E. Simon Jr. to understand that he's a man who regards the status quo as a challenge. It's little wonder that he's the father of Reston—a rare person who possesses a practical, analytical mind balanced with vision and an aptitude for business. And yes, when I asked him if he remained active, his response: "I just ran for a position on our condo board and won."

Published by *Grapevine* magazine
Robert E. Simon passed away in September 2015 at age 101.

Chapter 21

KENNETH CULBERT

2000

Mr. Kenneth Culbert, principal of Loudoun Valley High School in Purcellville, holds forth every school day morning in the lobby. He knows many of the 1,500 students by name, as he signed a signature-filled T-shirt for some cause or other. "It's Molly, isn't it? Good luck at Harmony next year."

Culbert has a reputation as one who practices discipline. "I believe that every action has consequences, that punishment should be swift, proportional, meaningful, impersonal. We try to instill that you should represent yourself, your family, your school and your community. Discipline can't be all negative. Has to end on a positive note, and it needs to have an end."

Eeda Dennis of the Leesburg Garden Club presented Culbert with a special award this year for the landscaping of the school grounds—done by the students.

> *Yes, we have a number of projects like that. We try to make them ongoing so they can be passed from class to class. The English students created the Shakespeare Garden; Window on the Wild by the Naturalist Society; and others have done the landscaping around the school. We have had the history students photograph the Heritage Trail, and the Saturday before Mother's Day, the students mulch, weed and tend the grounds. We also have a learning laboratory where we bring in elementary students. It makes them more aware of their environment.*

This page: Kenneth Culbert. *Photo by Bob Updegrove.*

He believes that athletics build confidence and give the kids a healthy taste of life. "You get knocked down by someone you don't even know, and you have to pick yourself up and keep going. And you often have to stretch yourself beyond what you thought your capabilities were. But it's not just athletics. Drama, for example, having to get up in front of people and perform."

The inevitable question of the events at Columbine comes up. "Society has changed in the last quarter century," he says. "In many homes, both Mom and Dad work, and direct supervision is left up to the young person until Mom and Dad get home pretty tired. We've seen a reduction of pure family activities. The divorce rate has gone way up, with sometimes resulting anger and families torn apart. The kids carry these burdens to school."

He pulls out a device, pushes a button and sounds an alarm. "This is our bellybuttonometer." He hands an abashed young lady a piece of duct tape with which to hide the offending midriff.

Why does he sit out here every morning? "Several reasons," he says. "I like to, for one thing. It gives me a chance to mingle with the students. I think it's important for me to be visible, to see what's going on and to have the students be comfortable with me." He interrupts himself: "Jennifer…."

Then he has to leave, and he trundles off down the hallway in his wheelchair to mix with his students and faculty. He calls over his shoulder, "If you have a camera, be sure and take a picture of our wild turkeys in the Window on the Wild garden…" his voice trailing off.

I spoke with two senior girls. What about Mr. Culbert? "We respect him so much," they say. And why is that? "He gives us respect right back. It's a mutual thing. He loves us and cares about us, and he makes school interesting….and he keeps us in line." Afraid? "Only when he sounds the bellybuttonometer," they say, giggling. A faculty member confirms his strength: "His rapport with the students."

I don't wonder that in years from now, the class reunions will be talking about Kenneth Culbert with respect and affection.

Mr. Culbert explained how he disciplined students. He would tell them that they represented not only themselves but also their community, family and school. He said he would always

end on a positive note after admonishing the student for what
he had done.

Published in *Loudoun Times Mirror*
*Kenneth Culbert passed away in December 2003 after serving thirty-seven years in the
Loudoun County School System.*

Chapter 22

BRUCE SMART

2013

I followed Bruce Smart's directions by driving to Round Hill from Leesburg and then went left on Route 719 for a few miles before turning right on Trappe Road. The air was fresh and clean after a deluge the day before. Some of the gravel road had been rutted with the runoff. The drive along 719 and Trappe Road can be described as Loudoun County's finest and most rustic. Farmland with rolling pastoral scenes spotted with grazing cattle, sheep and horses, stables, farmhouses and stacks of hay, all bordered by stone walls, spreads in every direction. I knew for sure that I had entered the heart of equine country.

Bruce Smart and his wife, Edith, raise Thoroughbreds, and at age ninety, Bruce can look back on a distinguished international career in government and private industry while enjoying his authorship of a trilogy of books on the horse community. The latest one, called *A Community of the Horse: Legacies*, has been met with praise. As one reviewer put it, it "draws us gracefully and passionately into the world of horses, horsemen and women, horse sports, art, literature, and the places they share."

One of the chapters particularly carries with it a pictorial display of the horse community. The paintings by local equine artists give testament to how alive this community is and what it means to a host of people.

Bruce began to describe some of the paintings as we sat in his parlor and leafed through the book. He selected these particular artists as, for him, they gave definition to the equine world. About his book, he said, "I'm a reporter, not a creative writer, and I write stuff based on that." He went on to say, "Doing these books is wonderful because you get to know people."

Bruce Smart. *Photo by Joe Motheral.*

He likes Linda Volrath, the artist who did the painting on the cover of his book titled *Into the Foothills*. Bruce said, "You have the sky and countryside, the horse dutifully towing a cart, a traditional style of transportation." The horse-drawn cart shows "our dependence on equine transport, pre-automobile." Bruce noted, "The guy [is] dressed appropriately for the countryside. Not dressed like some fancy guy at a horse show. It brought people beautifully back to the relationship between man and horse. They are connected through the reins. Not a fancy horse."

In addition to the horse and cart, Linda Volrath made a painting of the horses at Oatlands and another Bruce likes called *The Blue Pages*. Here again, this painting expresses a semblance of action. Volrath is a prolific painter, with some twenty paintings a year she creates for the Sporting Gallery in Middleburg. She began at an early age and graduated from the Art Institute of Philadelphia. The Torpedo Factory in Alexandria gave her access to the gallery there.

Bruce gives deceased self-taught artist Jean Bowman a big thumbs up as a skilled local painter and one who fits his concept of good equine art. "I would look for emotion; I would like to see action. I don't particularly like portraits, not as good as action. Feeling emotion has become more appealing than the classical." He defines emotion as the connection between horse and human.

Bowman's paintings include *A Practice*, with horse and rider against a backdrop of farmlike countryside. It was her approach to beginning a painting. She expanded that by filling in additional elements into one titled *The Meadow Brook Hounds* with horses, hounds and hunters preparing for a fox hunt. Another of Bruce's favorites paintings is Winkie Mackay-Smith of the horse Farnley Ensign. "It's a horse and rider returning to the stables."

As is obvious from the collection, Bruce prefers realism to, say, impressionism. Perhaps the one closest to an impressionistic form is Peggy Arundel's *A Beginner of a Yearling*. She was studying under Sandra Forbush, who painted the one of the little girl dressed in "master's" garb surrounded by foxhounds, titled *Practicing to Be Master of the Foxhounds*. He says Sandra is one of his favorite artists, describing her as more literal in her style. She was another one who began drawing at an early age and progressed with her love of horses and her proximity to them.

We took a tour of the Smart farm, which spreads across the upslope of the foothills near Upperville. Several horses grazing added to the breadth of the scene. I asked Bruce how he got interested in horses. "My father was a horse guy. A very athletic man; had polio when he was two years old. He couldn't count on running. So he went to horses. Learned to play polo. So my sister and I each had a horse."

I asked Bruce how he started writing his trilogy, the first being *A Community of the Horse: Relationships*, about folks within the horse community. He said, "When we first moved into the area, we used to go to parties and found people were bonded together by a common interest, and I asked folks why people liked horses and wrote on cocktail napkins. Next thing I knew, I had fifty cocktail napkins."

The second book, *Community of the Horse: Stakes and Stake Holders*, is about "horse breeders and owners."

He says his wife, Edith, grew up with horses and became a foxhunter. When they got married, both declared, "Someday, we are going to have horses."

———

Bruce Smart served as undersecretary of commerce before retiring to raise Thoroughbreds and write books.

———

Published in *elan* magazine
You can buy Bruce Smart's books at the National Sporting Library and Museum in Middleburg, Virginia. He and Edith lived in Upperville at 20561 Trappe Road with Thoroughbreds and his stash of books. They once owned the horse Flower Alley, which sired Derby winner I'll Have Another. Bruce passed away in November 2018.

Chapter 23

JOE MAY

2022

At age eighty-four, Joe May's career spans a length of time that is replete with achievements and honors of storybook proportions. According to reports from the Academy of Engineering Excellence, Joe May always had a knack for electrical engineering and science. During his three years in the army, he spent a year in electronics school. He later enrolled at Virginia Tech and earned a degree in electrical engineering in 1962. He founded an electronic company named EIT in 1977. In addition to his tour in the business world, earning twenty-eight patents, he served twenty years in the Virginia House of Delegates.

He had his eightieth birthday party at Belmont Country Club. Several hundred people—family, friends and colleagues—attended. He went through a PowerPoint presentation of his life. As he described the related events and milestones, he several times made reference to "the guys I worked with." He said that rather than "the guys who worked for me." It was an earmark of his humble character.

EIT has two hundred employees, and there is a display in the building with forty-six nations' flags. Joe said it represents their employees' countries of origin. I asked him what he thought was the crowning achievement of EIT, and he said, "Surviving and contributing for forty-six years." EIT's latest project has to do with the COVID virus. "We are adapting ultraviolet radiation sanitizer to disinfect things like hospital rooms, clinics—just about anything to kill COVID."

Perhaps one of his most visible landmarks is the orange line designating the first down line on the football field, as seen on TV. He recalled that it

Joe and Bobby May. *Photo provided by Joe May.*

all started when Candlestick Park in San Francisco wanted to replace local advertising in a TV picture. Princeton Video Imaging retained EIT. Once they had accomplished that, Joe said, "they asked if we had some way of marking the first down line. We did the design work, we tested it and repaired it for quite a few years."

May says his motive for being elected to the Virginia House of Delegates related to his concern about computer laws: "Getting computer laws on some sort of reasonable track. Computer privacy was just a morass. They were able to steal anything about you they wanted to." His efforts contributed to what became the Computer Trespass Laws.

Joe and his wife, Bobby, have been married for over fifty years. He says, "I married my girlfriend's roommate." When asked how his wife contributed to his career he said, "Politics; she's a natural politician. I don't claim to be any of the above. She's courteous to people, she's a good listener."

Prior to his founding EIT, he says, "I spent a couple years as a self-employed consultant. I designed two instruments for the DuPont Company. They encouraged me to start EIT and offered to help."

Some of his latest accomplishments include developing an instrument to determine the distance from a helicopter in flight to the ground. "We based it on a Mercedes radar device that measures the distance to the car in front." One of his more interesting assignments occurred when International Paper was referred to EIT by DuPont. He said they came to him with the question, "Can you tell us how to determine how much ink is on a bread wrap?" Joe says he wondered who would care. "It turns out that the people who make the wrappers care because of the cost of the ink. They needed that information so they could bid on a printing job." He ended up designing something to determine this, and "it turned out to be one of our most profitable."

As a form of off-street activity, Joe says their house is on six acres and they like to garden and watch TV reruns like *M*A*S*H*. And they like to travel with family members. Recently, they went to Africa.

He has earned prestigious awards; most recently, he was inducted into the Virginia Tech Academy of Engineering Excellence. He will undoubtedly earn more as time goes on. In 2000, he was honored with the Governor's Award for Technology.

Published in *Country Zest and Style* magazine
Thanks to Suzan and Vernon Davis.
EIT is located near Leesburg Airport. It has a shelter for a helicopter that Joe May can fly.

Chapter 24

DR. FAROUK EL BAZ

2022

Dr. Farouk El Baz lives with his wife, Patricia, in Leesburg. Originally from Egypt, he was a geologist on the Apollo Lunar Missions from 1967 to 1972. He and his colleagues determined the safest lunar landing sites.

Dr. Farouk was secretary of NASA's Landing Site Selection Committee, consisting of twenty-eight scientists. He developed the rationale for selecting a landing site and the scientific objectives of the six lunar landing missions. He chaired astronaut training in visual observations and photography and served at the Mission Operation Control Room at the L.B. Johnson Space Center at Clear Lake City, Texas. He and his team were successful in selecting all of the Apollo landing sites. He said, "It was especially satisfying, particularly because none of the participants had been there or experienced anything like it. It was even more so because I became a U.S. citizen in 1970."

He said, "We had no idea what it looked like and what we should seek there." NASA planned three unmanned missions, he said, "to transmit helpful information. Ranger was to crash on the moon to see how its surface behaves." The other two took multiple images of the moon's surface. "I concentrated my efforts on the two-thousand-plus images sent by Lunar Orbiter. I began to classify the lunar surface features and study their locations for landing site selection." Dr. Farouk's objective involved finding a "flat enough surface to allow the craft to land perfectly upright, which would ease a perfect launch at the end." And, he said, "we wanted it to be free of large blocks that might interfere with a safe landing."

Farouk El Baz. *Photo from Cairo archives.*

Astronaut Alfred Worden, recently deceased, recalled while circling the moon during Mission 15, "I feel like I've been here before."

Dr. Farouk became friends with all the astronauts, some of whom studied geology with his guidance. For example, he said that "David Scott, Apollo 45 commander, absorbed a great deal of geology. His wife even took some courses in geology saying, 'so that I could talk to him.'"

Farouk, one of nine children, was born on January 2, 1938, in Zagazig, Egypt. After high school, he attended Ain Shams University. He said, "There, I selected to study geology, as I had been fascinated by natural rock landforms on Boy Scout trips during school years."

In 1960, he was offered a scholarship for graduate study in the United States. "I was accepted at the Missouri School of Mines and Metallurgy in Rolla, Missouri." There, he earned a master's degree and PhD in geology that included one year at MIT. Soon afterward, he interviewed for a job on the Apollo Space Mission.

Dr. Farouk has received a number of awards, including the Egyptian Order of Merit, First Class, and the Apollo Achievement Award, among many others. He also has seven honorary doctoral degrees. He is a fellow of the U.S. Academy of Engineering and the Academy of Sciences for the Developing World, which he represents at the United Nations. And he has had a spacecraft named after him.

NASA Public Relations sent a film crew to cover one of his teaching exercises. The sound man on the crew was particularly interested in lunar features. He later became co-producer of *Star Trek: The Next Generation*. Dr. Farouk said, "When they needed a name for that shuttle, he suggested mine."

He is working on two books: "One on my improbable life journey and the other on my proof that my ancestors, the ancient Egyptians, selected the form of their monuments after natural landforms in their Western Desert."

Patricia and Farouk have four daughters and seven grandchildren.

Published in *Country Zest and Style* magazine

Chapter 25

JUDY HEISER

2022

Judy Heiser's career as an artist began some twenty years ago. But her artistic pattern came about long before that. She has been a professional dancer on stages around the world as a ballerina and choreographed dancer. When I asked her if that had anything to do with her becoming a painter, she said, "As a professional dancer for twenty years, dancing with a passion—I learned to paint with fearless passion, expression and movement. Like choreographing on an empty stage, I embrace a blank canvas and rehearse lines, making marks, changing lines, forms, shapes." Judy sees herself as an "action" painter, and when she and her family moved to Washington, D.C., she became entranced with the area and the art galleries.

By viewing her artwork, one can see, as she indicated, "I'm moved by subjects with interesting lighting, mood, atmosphere, earth, oceans, water, reflections, clouds, colors of the morning and evening skies and birds in flight." All of these ingredients can be seen in her paintings, which are on display at her studio in the Torpedo Factory Art Center in Alexandria. She pointed to one titled *Break of Dawn* that she says is a landscape scene in Maryland. The abstract version gives the painting a sense of mystery, and the colors she used have been extracted from nature. Others such as *Roads to Everywhere, Unstructured* and *Summer Splash* show intensity of color and substance.

Her worldview and artistic enthusiasm give her an endless supply of subjects to paint. "I'm inspired by the art of looking, curiosity and wonder, travel

Left: Judy Heiser. *Photo by Sarah Marcello*.

Below: Painting by Judy Heiser. *Photo by Sarah Marcello*.

and explorations." She explained further, "My initial conceptual baseline enthused from abstracting nature, research, observations, interpretations of stories, postures, moments and relationships." In order to release these emotions and the basics to engage in a painting, she said, "I paint outside as much as possible, although painting from my studio, I'm always looking out the window. My paintings are constantly changing."

Judy has had a multifaceted career as a dancer, on the staff at FEMA, motherhood and now her formidable passion: painting. She has workshops and accordingly enjoys teaching art and tells her students "to keep at it as long as you are having fun. Struggle with it." She says that her students give her incentives to look at art differently. She previously taught recreational art therapy at Mount Vernon Hospital; that has been interrupted by the COVID pandemic. She hopes to return to doing that soon. As a student herself, Judy attended the Corcoran College of Art and Design, as well as the Alexandria Art League.

Her journey into art began as a youngster when, she said, "I was always creative, drawing and painting, and I thought I would do that in college, but it wasn't taking off for me the way I wanted it to." So she began dancing instead. She said, "It was something I could do." Her devotion to painting has in no way taken her completely away from performing arts. She is involved with the Alexandria Community Theater, serving as a director, choreographer, set designer and more. In her words, "Performing arts and visual arts have my heart, and I love to teach and share whenever I can."

Her regimen as a painter involves the use of multiple mediums. As she says, she begins with "loose gestures, using mixed medium drawing tools." She often starts with a combination of charcoal and graphite sticks. She then can move on to layers of gesso, acrylics and encaustics, all of which are formulated by "color choices that are discovered intuitively." She says she works on several paintings at one time, going from one to the other. It can take her anywhere from one hour to eight months to complete a painting. Her work is predominantly abstract; that not only includes landscapes, but many of her paintings derive simply from her imagination and are occasionally of people, such as one titled *Can't Beat This* that was painted with beet juice and ink.

She looks into her future as engaging in teaching, and she would like to do more plein air. She says she will likely pull back a bit from abstract to more realism. Whatever the theme, you can count on Judy to immerse herself with intensity and passion.

Judy has just been accepted at the Nepenthe Gallery, "a brand-new one in Alexandria," she says. She was invited as guest speaker in their guest speaker series on May 5, 2022. Her paintings are also exhibited at the Coldwell Banker Realty for ArtSpire VA, a nonprofit organization. And, she says, "I am participating in charity for Alexandria's Children and Family Network Centers." Meanwhile, she continues her presence at the Torpedo Factory Art Center in Alexandria. Her paintings were being reviewed by a jury at Athenium Art Gallery in Alexandria.

Published in *elan* magazine

Chapter 26

REMEMBERING BILL BERRY

2016

In the early morning hours of Wednesday, December 14, 2016, the community and society in general lost Bill Berry, one of their most valued members. During the last few days of his life at Adler Center, Bill was surrounded by loved ones—his family and friends.

Bill Berry began his life in Tulsa, Oklahoma. He later attended college at Oklahoma University, where he obtained a business degree and took some courses in geology. After graduation, he joined the family business in the oil fields of Texas before turning his career into home building in Washington, D.C., and the suburbs, including Loudoun County. His modesty and quiet reserve gave little notice of his lifetime achievements. He won numerous home design awards, served his community in social causes and occasionally found camaraderie on the golf course, not to mention his attending weekly tai chi lessons for one year.

I sat with him and his life partner, Pat Kalinsky, once to discuss his career. He related that after the oil and gas business in Texas suffered a downturn because of the oil boom in the Middle East, he shifted gears in 1966 and became a "trainee" with a developer in Northern Virginia. He explained, "There are similarities between the oil and gas business and real estate development. Buying oil leases and mineral rights is a form of real estate."

His entrepreneurial bent came from family and relatives, most of whom had their own businesses. So after he arrived in this area, he rapidly moved up in the organization he had joined. His big break came when he prepared a business plan suggesting selling apartments owned by the development

Bill Berry. *Photo by Joe Motheral.*

company he worked for and then acquiring open land to build homes. After that, he went out on his own and founded the Berry Companies, which over the years built thousands of homes mostly in Virginia and Maryland, including some eighty patio homes and twenty-five single-family dwellings in River Creek.

"There are three things that make success in the housing market: better location, a lower per-square-foot price and exciting designs." He and Pat mentioned that they went against advice from local realtors who told him that compartmentalized rooms were the ticket. Instead, his homes, he said, typically have "volume, light views and openness." Indeed, when you walk into one, you are greeted with high ceilings and "something interesting in every direction," including an open vista throughout most of the house.

Bill had a social conscience that exceeded standard boundaries. Just to name a few, he was on the board of LAWS (Loudoun Abused Women's Shelter); he founded AHOME (Affordable Housing Opportunity Means Everyone) and subsequently was inducted into the AHOME Hall of Fame. His concern about the homeless and housing for everyone drove him to Richmond, where he lobbied for less restrictive limits on locating low-income housing. His concerns weren't related only to housing. He once raised funds for Montgomery County American Cancer Society. According to a member of the Synagogue, "He was passionate about his faith and helped add a sanctuary and classrooms at the Temple Emanuel." He told me that one time, he went to Israel in hopes of finding oil.

His many accomplishments, however, don't outweigh how fond people were of him. Ask anyone about Bill Berry, and they always say simply, "He's a nice man."

The content was taken from an interview with Bill Berry in 2012 plus information from his obituary in the Washington Post.
Published in *Loudoun Times Mirror*

Chapter 27

BAZIL NEWMAN

2005

In 2002, a resident of River Creek, a gated community located between the Potomac River and Goose Creek, found a tombstone resting beside a tree. The inscription on the stone tablet reads, "Bazil Newman departed this life July 8, 1852 at the age of 72 years nine months." According to information at the Balch Library in Leesburg, Newman was the boatman on Edwards Ferry, and his family cemetery, as shown on the county cemetery map, is located within the River Creek community along Olympic Boulevard. The River Creek HOA maintains the cemetery.

The U.S. Census of 1850 recorded Bassell [*sic*] Newman, Black, as head of the household. Basil [*sic*] Newman in 1835 purchased 119 acres of land along Goose Creek. The attendant at the Balch Library said, "That meant he couldn't have been a slave. He had to have been free to have owned land."

The developer of River Creek, Marc Montgomery, had the stone set in concrete, put up a plaque and sponsored a dedication ceremony in February 2008. Pauline Singletary, the chairperson of the Loudoun County Black History Committee, attended and commented, "We think that Bazil Newman was part of the Underground Railroad, transporting escaped Black slaves across the river into Maryland, where they went on to points north." There is evidence that Philadelphia abolitionists listed names of Loudoun slaves in the city.

Bazil Newman eventually owned 186 acres within the 500-plus acres of present-day River Creek. He farmed the land, apparently raising grain, probably wheat. But he didn't neglect operating the ferry. Sometime around

1839, he ran an ad in the *Genius of Liberty* newspaper announcing that he "may always be found at his post and the most careful."

According to records from the Balch Library, William Shreve, a white man, had a warehouse constructed in 1839 on the east side of Goose Creek across from the land that Newman had purchased in 1835. Shreve immediately placed several ads in Leesburg's weekly *Genius of Liberty.* "Bazil Newman, well known as an old and experienced boatman, who will attend at the warehouse to receive and forward goods." At some point, Newman joined two others in the ownership of Elizabeth Mill, located along Goose Creek.

This being the period before railroads, goods were transported via waterways. Just downstream from where Goose Creek enters the Potomac are the remnants of a set of locks that were used to hoist boats up and onto the Chesapeake and Ohio Canal. It afforded opportunities for the warehouse to send grain into the Washington, D.C. area.

Records at the Balch Library indicate Newman was born in November 1779 and by 1820 had a household composed of "white companion and housekeeper." He eventually added three sons, Basil, Benjamin and Robert. Benjamin carried on the family tradition by operating Edwards Ferry after his father's passing. A search is underway to try to locate present-day relatives of Bazil Newman.

Chapter 28

OTHERS OF NOTE

I have been fortunate to be able to interview and write about some of the people in Northern Virginia who have gained at least a modicum of distinction. There are three others that come to mind—ones whom I have had the misfortune of not having the opportunity to interview. In some cases, they are deceased.

In another case, there may someday be an opportunity. I'm referring to Robert Duvall, who lives near The Plains, Virginia. His movie career has made him an icon not only of Northern Virginia but worldwide as well. I still remember his first movie, *To Kill a Mockingbird*, in which he plays the part of Boo Radley. He once owned a restaurant in The Plains called the Rail Stop. At the time, there were photos on the wall of scenes from some of his movies. He is no longer the owner, and unfortunately, the photos have been taken down.

We did have an opportunity to meet when Alan Geoffrion—who wrote the screenplay for *Broken Trail* with Duvall in the lead—was one of the authors at the National Press Club Book Fair and brought Duvall. When he stepped off the elevator, you immediately knew who he was. He was very cordial. Many of the staff at the Press Club are Hispanic, and Duvall chatted with them in Spanish.

Madeleine Albright had a farm in Northern Virginia. I had an opportunity to meet her when she came to Leesburg once to campaign for Kelly Burk, who was running for town council at the time and is now mayor of Leesburg. I spoke with Albright's assistant and asked about scheduling an interview.

She seemed somewhat positive, but it never happened, unfortunately. Albright was very pleasant. According to stories circulating, she used to eat occasionally at the Planet Wayside Restaurant in Hamilton. She was secretary of state at the time and had bodyguards. Once, she left her purse at the restaurant, and her bodyguards found it while she was driving away. They had to call her to return.

According to Wikipedia, Vinton and Robert Pickens bought the property now occupied by the Janelia Campus of the Howard Hughes Medical Institute in 1934 and built a house in 1936. He was a reporter with Associated Press, and they were living in Switzerland at the time.

Vinton Pickens's countywide fame resulted from her founding the Loudoun County Planning Commission in 1941. She was an artist and was instrumental in promoting the highway signage ordinance—no billboards—that exists today in Loudoun County. She worked on that issue with Russell Baker's uncle, who chaired the board of supervisors. "He was my father's older brother," said Baker.

Eeda Dennis, as mentioned previously, was a longtime resident of Loudoun County and has been a constant source of past knowledge. She knew Mrs. Pickens and described her as "charming, no nonsense and down to facts." In other words, Pickens dealt in facts, not hearsay or speculation. Dennis said that Pickens was a good friend of General George C. Marshall and that "she served tea every afternoon at 4:00 p.m. and that she simply could not say no to anyone who wanted to use her home for, say, an art exhibit or reception selling jewelry, whatever."

In 1944, Pickens founded what was then known as Hot Sketchers (now the Loudoun Sketch Club), which features local artists and their work.

She sold her property to the Howard Hughes Medical Institute (HHMI), and in keeping with the Preservation and Scenic Easement, HHMI maintains the Pickens home and has observed the stipulation that there should be an unobstructed view of Sugarloaf Mountain.

According to Dennis, Pickens sold the property originally to a realtor in Washington, D.C., who eventually sold it to HHMI. Her house remains following her death without occupants.

The captains of fate must have been at work to form a collaborative match between a person like Howard Hughes and Pickens, a local activist and artist, to have had a hand in developing an institute that studies and produces medical research for the good of humankind. And the name Janelia? The Pickenses had two daughters, one named Jane and the other Cornelia. Janelia is a combination of the two.

The well-known best-selling author David Baldacci is another resident of Northern Virginia. I tried several times to get an interview, but he is constantly tied up with his writing, book events and the firm he founded, Wishing You Well Foundation, which combats illiteracy in the United States. According to information gleaned from the internet, his mother started his writing by giving him spiral notebooks at an early age. He publishes two books a year. I attended one of his book events hawking a book with military-type activity—parachuting and an obstacle course. A person in the audience asked how he did his research, and Baldacci replied that he personally engages. In other words, he jumped out of a plane with a parachute and pushed himself through an obstacle course.

Ethel and Robert Kennedy once lived off Kirby Road in McLean. One day, a neighbor drove by their house and reported that he saw Robert Kennedy dangling from the rooftop of his house wielding a paintbrush.

Any more?

Of course, there are a number of others—too many to name. I've been fortunate to have met a few. For example, Jim Lehrer, who for years was on

Jim Lehrer and Geraldine Brooks with the author at the National Press Club Book Fair. *Courtesy of Joe Motheral.*

TV broadcasting for Public Broadcasting System (PBS). He wrote books and often was one of the authors at the National Press Club's annual Book Fair. He was a big fan of George C. Marshall and gave a talk in Leesburg as a guest of the George C. Marshall International Center. Lehrer passed away in 2021.

Vicky Moon, in her book *Middleburg Mystique*, writes that Jackie Kennedy (who enjoyed fox hunting), Averill and Pamela Harriman, Elizabeth Taylor, Tab Hunter, Robert Wagner, Oliver North and several others have lived or spent time in the Middleburg area.

And in the political and public service arena, Rachel Flynn serves as deputy county executive in Fairfax County. She has a staff of 1,750 and is involved in planning and development, land development services, transportation, public works and environmental services and more. She handles a budget of $300 million for operations and $5 billion for capital improvement projects. She says that her most daunting task is "to transform Fairfax County from an automobile-dependent place to one where walking, biking and transit use are more common."

Finally, James Dickey, the author of the book *Deliverance*, wrote the first draft while living in Leesburg in the 1960s. He was also the Library of Congress poet laureate.

ABOUT THE AUTHOR

Joe Motheral and his wife, Marjorie, have lived in Northern Virginia for twenty-five years. He has written for a number of publications over a period of fifty years. He has over two hundred stories in print, past and present, including writing weekly columns for *Lawrence Eagle Tribune*, being a stringer for *Abilene Reporter News*, being a columnist for the *Loudoun Times Mirror*, being a close-up editor for *Grapevine* magazine and writing stories for an assortment of regional magazines, including *elan, Ashburn, Eastern Home and Travel, Loudouner* and *Country Zest and Style*. He and Linda Hendrickson published a children's book titled *Curly the Llama*. He has been the co-chairperson of the Book and Author Committee at the National Press Club.

He spent twenty-eight years overseas with his wife and family—in Abu Dhabi, Kuwait, Bangkok and Taiwan—for an engineering company. As such, he covered the Middle East and East Asia. He wrote a book about the Middle East (not published) with each chapter about a different country and is working on another book about World War II.